The Essential Instant Pot Cookbook

Top 200 Deliciously Simple and Easy Recipes for Your Instant Pot Pressure Cooker

By

Emma Hamilton

Copyright © 2019 by Emma Hamilton

All Right Reserved. No part of this publication may be reproduced, distributed, or transmitted in any form or by any means, including photocopying, recording, or other electronic or mechanical methods, or by any information storage and retrieval system without the prior written permission of the copyright holder.

Effort has been made to ensure that the information in this book is accurate and complete, however, the author and the publisher do not warrant the accuracy of the information, text and graphics contained within the book due to the rapidly changing nature of science, research, known and unknown facts and internet. The Author and the publisher do not hold any responsibility for errors, omissions or contrary interpretation of the subject matter herein. This book is presented solely for motivational and informational purposes only.

Table Of Contents

Introduction 1
Breakfast Recipes 2
    Orange Steel Cut Oats 2
    Steamed Eggs 2
    Egg Muffins 2
    Mini Frittatas 3
    Chile Colorado Smothered Burritos 3
    Scotch Eggs 4
    Blueberry Steel Cut Oats 4
    I P Hardboiled Eggs 5
    Mac and Cheese 5
    Baked Chicken 6
    Savory Mushroom Thyme Oatmeal 6
    Beef Brisket 7
    Cinnamon Roll Steel Cut Oats 7
    Apple Sauce 8
    Breakfast Quinoa 8
    Crust less Quiche 8
    Chicken Walking Tacos 9
    Cream and Berries Breakfast Cake 9
    Almond Steel Cut Oats 10
    Eggs de Provence 10
    Crust less Tomato Spinach Quiche 11
    Sausage and Peppers 11
    Cherry Apple Risotto 12
    Steel Cut Oats 12
    Carrot Cake Oatmeal 13
    Chicken Tacos 13
    Strawberries Steel Cut Oats 14
    Buffalo Chicken 14
    Apple Steel Cut Oats 14
    Cranberry Bake French Toast 15
Lunch Recipes 16

Root Beer Pull Pork Sandwiches 16

Chicken Lettuce Wraps 16

Chicken Tinga 17

Teriyaki Chicken Wings 17

Cola Chicken Wings 18

Cheesy Noodles 18

Tex Mex Chili Mac 19

Barbeque Bacon Apple Chicken 19

Santa Fe Chicken 20

Wheat Berry Salad 20

Chicken Cacciatore 21

Chicken Marsala 21

Barbeque Chicken Strip Salad 22

Indian Butter Chicken 23

Chicken Parmesan Meatballs in Ranch Sauce 23

French Dip Sandwiches 24

Salmon and Rice with Lemon Caper Chimichurri 24

Summer Garden Boiled Peanut Salad 25

Salsa Verde Chicken 25

Pork Carnitas Burrito Bowls 26

Pork Tamales 27

Spanish Brown Rice 28

Moroccan Sticky Chicken 28

Pork Vindaloo 29

Bahn Mi Sliders 29

Sirloin Tips in Gravy 30

Sloppy Lasagna 31

Salsa Lime Chicken with Mozzarella 32

Korean Beef 32

Cauliflower Fettuccine Alfredo 33

Coq Au Vin 33

Shredded Beef Enchiladas 34

Merlot Beef and Vegetables 35

Dinner Recipes 36

Mongolian Beef 36

Sausage and Pasta 36

Cranberry Beef Roast 37

Sweet and Sour Meatballs 37

Apple Pie Pork Chops 38

Barbeque Ribs 38

Italian Beef 38

Pulled Pork Loaded Sweet Potatoes 39

Meatballs 39

Braised Short Ribs 40

Osso Bucco 40

Corned Beef and Cabbage 41

Turkey with Gravy 41

Rack of Lamb Casserole 42

Marinated Steak 42

Lamb Shanks with Figs and Ginger 42

General Tso's Shredded Chicken 43

Pot Roast 44

Beef Rouladen 44

Cranberry Maple Orange Pork Chops 45

Arroz Con Pollo 45

Awesome Sweet and Sour Spare Ribs 46

Ranch Pork Chops 47

Jambalaya 47

Citrus Herb Chicken 47

Country Steak 48

Carnitas 48

Orange Adobo Chicken 48

Spiced Cranberry Pot Roast 49

Duck with Vegetables 49

Brown Sugar Garlic Chicken 50

Cherry Apple Pork Loin 50

Bourbon Honey Chicken 50

Creamy Italian Chicken Recipe 51

Cream Cheese Chicken ... 51

Shrimp and Pork Dumplings ... 51

Honey Chicken ... 52

Beer Potato Fish ... 52

Honey Glazed Chicken Thighs ... 53

Barbeque Hawaiian Turkey Meatloaf ... 53

Roast Chicken ... 54

Coconut Chicken Curry ... 54

Herb Buttermilk Chicken ... 55

Harvest Ham Dinner ... 55

Coconut Tofu Curry ... 55

Braised Duck with Potato ... 56

Maple Mustard Chicken ... 56

Chicken Parmigiana ... 56

Soups, Sides and Snacks Recipes ... 57

Mexican Style Chicken Soup ... 57

Chorizo Chili ... 57

Curried Coconut Chicken Soup ... 58

Tomato Basil and Beef Soup ... 58

Hamburger Barley Vegetable Soup ... 59

Jalapeno Popper Chicken Chili ... 59

Split Pea with Ham Soup ... 60

Creamy Tomato Soup ... 60

African Style Chickpea Coconut Soup ... 60

Sweet and Spicy Red Beans ... 61

White Bean Chili Chicken ... 61

Hearty Beef Stew ... 61

Beef and Porcini Mushroom Stew ... 62

Lentil Vegetable Soup ... 62

Taco Soup ... 63

Chicken Noodle Soup ... 63

Sweet Potato Soup ... 64

Macaroni Soup ... 64

Beef Stew with Turnips and Carrots ... 65

Pork Shank Carrots Soup ... 65
Healthy Chili ... 66
Tuscan Chicken Stew ... 66
Potato Soup ... 67
Bean Soup with Pork ... 67
Pork Rib and Lotus Root Soup ... 68
Winter Minestrone ... 68
Rice and Chicken Ranch Soup ... 68
Seared Marinated Artichokes ... 69
Mango Dal ... 69
Spicy Chicken Soup ... 70
Pho Ga ... 70
Sweet Carrot Puree ... 71
Potato Risotto ... 71
Smoky Ham Hock and Pinto Bean Soup ... 72
Cheesy Potato Soup ... 72
Orange Brussels Sprouts ... 72
Baked Potatoes ... 73
Corn On the Cob ... 73
Black Eyed Pea Soup ... 73
Savory Spaghetti Sauce with Bacon ... 74
Awesome Mexican Green Rice ... 74
Maple Bacon Acorn Squash ... 75
Zuppa Toscana ... 75
Corn Chowder ... 76
Taco Chicken Soup ... 76
Pumpkin Chicken Corn Chowder ... 77
Garlic Mushrooms with White Beans and Farro ... 77

Dessert Recipes ... 78

Steamed Carrot Pudding Cake ... 78
Black Chocolate Cake ... 78
Black Rice Pudding with Dried Cherries ... 79
Raisin Bread Pudding with Caramel Pecan Sauce ... 79
Pina Colada Rice Pudding ... 80

- Orange Swirl Cheesecake ... 80
- Pumpkin Chocolate Chip Bundt Cake ... 81
- Candied Lemon Peels ... 82
- Peanut Butter Cup Cheesecake ... 82
- Delicious Pumpkin Pie ... 83
- Cheesecake with Toffee Pecan Shortbread Cookie Crust ... 84
- Mango Coconut Rice Pudding ... 84
- Key Lime Pie ... 85
- Chocolate Pots de Creme ... 85
- Dulce de Leche ... 86
- Fruit Yogurt ... 86
- Poached Pears with Chocolate Sauce ... 87
- Polenta ... 87
- Tapioca Pudding ... 88
- Cheese Flan ... 88
- Robin Egg Mini Cheesecakes ... 89
- Heart Shaped Cheesecake ... 89
- Berry Compote ... 90
- Rice Pudding ... 91
- Coconut Lemongrass Ginger Tapioca ... 91
- Steamed Bread Pudding ... 92
- Raspberry Curd ... 92
- Date Pumpkin Brown Rice Pudding ... 93
- Triple Chocolate Layered Cheesecake ... 93
- Creme Brulee Cheesecake Bites ... 94
- Meyer Lemon Cheese cake ... 95
- Pumpkin Creme Brulee ... 96
- Apple Sauce ... 96

Introduction

The Instant Pot is the modern version of a traditional pressure cooker. It can braise, boil, pressure cook, sauté, shallow-fry, slow cook, and steam dishes all in one pot. It can cook everything from simple porridges to quick savory snacks to desserts. With the help of the Instant Pot and its numerous cooking functions, healthy dishes can be prepared, cooked, and served in less than an hour, and with only five ingredients— or less!

The cookbook you are holding in your hands contains 200 mouth-watering Instant Pot recipes that you can prepare using your Instant Pot. This book features easy to follow steps and strategies on how to use the Instant Pot to come up with a variety of great recipes. It contains recipes that are healthy, quick and easy to follow.

This book will make you feel more comfortable, not only using your pressure cooker but also making tasty, healthy meals. Everyone, regardless of diet, can be a part of the pressure cooker revolution, and this book proves it! So, whether you are new to pressure cooking, or are already an expert and simply want new recipes, we've got you covered. Come on, let's get cooking!

Breakfast Recipes

Orange Steel Cut Oats

[Servings: 6]

Ingredients:

- 1 cup Steel Cut Oats
- ½ cup Dried Cranberries
- 2 cups of Whole Milk
- 2 cups of Water
- ½ cup Orange [Juiced]
- 2 tbsp. Orange [Zested]
- 2 tbsp. Butter
- 1 tbsp. Maple Syrup
- ½ tsp. Vanilla Extract
- ½ tsp. Cinnamon

Directions:

1. Combine all of ingredients in glass oven-safe bowl. Mix together well. Add 1 cup water to your Instant Pot and place the trivet on top.
2. Place bowl on the trivet, lock lid into place and seal the steam nozzle
3. Cook on the Manual setting for approximately 6 minutes. Release the pressure naturally for a minimum of 10 minutes. Stir dried cranberries in and mix together well. Serve

Steamed Eggs

[Servings: 2]

Ingredients:

- 2 Large Eggs
- ½ cup Cold Water
- Chopped Scallions
- Pinch of Sesame Seeds
- Pinch of Garlic Powder
- Pinch of Salt
- Pinch of Pepper

Directions:

1. Begin by mixing eggs in a bowl. Pour eggs into heatproof bowl and add the rest of ingredients. Make sure you mix them together well. Set to the side
2. Add 1 cup water in your Instant Pot and place steamer basket in it. Place egg mixture into bowl. Close the lid and vent the valve
3. Cook with Manual on High pressure and set the timer for approximately 5 minutes with a Natural pressure release. Once finished cooking remove from Instant Pot. Serve.

Egg Muffins

[Servings: 4]

Ingredients:

- 4 Eggs
- 4 slices of Pre-Cooked Bacon [Crumbled]
- 1 Diced Green Onion
- ¼ tsp. Lemon Pepper Seasoning
- 4 tbsp. Shredded Cheddar/Jack Cheese

Directions:

1. Put steamer basket in your Instant Pot and add 1 ½ cups of water. Break eggs into a large-sized measuring bowl with a pour spout. Add lemon pepper and beat well.
2. Divide cheese, bacon and green onion evenly between 4 silicone muffin cups. Pour beaten eggs into each muffin cup and stir with fork to combine.

3. Place muffin cups in steamer basket. Cover and lock the lid in place. Select High pressure and cook for approximately 8 minutes
4. When the timer beeps, turn off, wait approximately 2 minutes, then use the Quick pressure release. Carefully open lid. Lift out steamer basket and remove the muffin cups. Serve.

Mini Frittatas

[Servings: 6]

Ingredients:

- ½ cup Almond Milk
- 5 Eggs
- Salt
- Pepper

Optional Toppings:

- Cheese
- Meat
- Vegetables

Directions:

1. Begin by mixing eggs, cheese, milk, salt, pepper, cheese, vegetables and meats. Use favorite baking molds and pour mixture in. Pour a cup water in your Instant Pot and place molds on the rack.
2. Cook on Manual with High pressure for approximately 5 minutes. Once cooked, use the Quick pressure release. Serve

Chile Colorado Smothered Burritos

[Servings: 4]

Ingredients:

- 3 lbs. of Boneless Beef Rump Roast [Cubed]
- 16 ounces of Enchilada Sauce [Divided]
- 2 Beef Bouillon Cubes
- 12 Burrito-Size Flour Tortillas
- 2 cups of Shredded Cheese
- ½ cup Water

Directions:

1. Add beef, enchilada sauce, bouillon and water to Instant Pot. Select High pressure and set the timer for approximately 30 minutes
2. When the beep sounds, turn off the Instant Pot and use a Natural pressure release for 10 minutes and then do a Quick pressure release to release any of the remaining pressure. When the valve drops carefully remove the lid
3. Put tortilla on a rimmed baking tray lined with aluminum foil. Add approximately ½ cup beef to the center of tortilla, fold in the edges and roll up into a burrito. Repeat with remaining tortillas. Top with enchilada sauce and shredded cheese. Broil until cheese is bubbly. Should take approximately 2 to 4 minutes. Serve.

Scotch Eggs

[Servings: 4]

Ingredients:

- 1 lb. of Country Style Ground Sausage
- 4 Large Eggs
- 1 tbsp. Vegetable Oil

Directions:

1. Put steamer basket in Instant Pot. Add 1 cup water and eggs. Lock the lid in place and cook on High pressure for approximately 6 minutes. When the timer beeps, let the pressure release naturally for about 6 minutes. Then turn off your Instant Pot and do a Quick pressure release.
2. When the pressure is released, carefully remove lid. Remove steamer basket from the Instant Pot. Put eggs into ice cold water to cool. When eggs are cool remove their shells. Divide sausage into four equal-sized pieces. Flatten each piece into a flat round. Place hard boiled egg in the center and gently wrap sausage around the egg.
3. Heat your Instant Pot on Sauté. When pot is hot, add oil and brown Scotch eggs on four sides. Remove Scotch eggs from the Instant Pot and add 1 cup water. Put a rack in your Instant Pot and place Scotch eggs on the rack.
4. Lock the lid in place and pressure cook on High pressure for approximately 6 minutes. When the timer beeps, do a Quick pressure release. When all of the pressure is released, carefully remove lid. Serve.

Blueberry Steel Cut Oats

[Servings: 4]

Ingredients:

- 1 cup Steel Cut Oats
- ½ cup Half and Half
- 3 cups of Water
- 1 cup Fresh or Frozen Blueberries
- ¼ cup Chia Seeds
- 1 tbsp. Lemon Zest
- 1 tbsp. Butter
- 2 tbsp. Sugar
- ¼ tsp. Salt

Optional Toppings:

- Sliced Almonds
- Milk
- Blueberries
- Honey

Directions:

1. Add butter to your Instant Pot and select Sauté. When butter is melted add oats and toast, stirring constantly, until they smell nutty. Should take approximately 3 minutes. Add water, sugar, half and half, lemon zest and salt. Select High pressure and cook for approximately 10 minutes.
2. When the beep sounds, turn off your Instant Pot and use a Natural pressure release for about 10 minutes and then do a Quick pressure release to release any of the remaining pressure. When the valve drops carefully remove the lid
3. Stir oats. Stir in blueberries and chia seeds. Cover and allow it to sit for 5 minutes until oats are the desired thickness. Top with additional blueberries, sliced almonds, honey and a splash of milk. Serve.

I P Hardboiled Eggs

[Servings: -]

Ingredients:

- Eggs [However Many You Prefer]
- 1 cup Water

Directions:

1. Pour water into pot and place eggs in steamer basket if you have one. If you don't, use the rack that came with Instant Pot. Close lid and set for approximately 5 minutes at High pressure
2. It will take cooker approximately 5 minutes to build to pressure and then another 5 minutes to cook. I allow the pressure to naturally reduce for another 5 minutes after the cooking cycle has completed, followed by a Quick pressure release. That's approximately 15 minutes in total. Place hot eggs into cool water to halt the cooking process. You can peel eggs immediately or wait. Serve.

Mac and Cheese

[Servings: 5]

Ingredients:

- 16 ounces of Elbow Macaroni
- 6 ounces of Freshly Grated Mild Cheddar or American Cheese
- 14 ounces of Freshly Grated Sharp Cheddar Cheese
- 4 cups of Cold Running Water
- 4 tbsp. Unsalted Butter
- Kosher Salt
- Ground Black pepper

Wet Ingredients:

- 2 Large Eggs [Beaten]
- 12-ounce can of Evaporated Milk
- 1 tsp. Ground Mustard
- 1 tsp. Sriracha Sauce or Frank's Hot Sauce

Directions:

1. Add 1 pound of elbow macaroni, 4 cups of water and a pinch of kosher salt to Instant Pot. Close the lid and cook at High pressure for approximately 4 minutes. Then use a gradual Quick release
2. There is a slight chance that a tiny amount of foam will come out with the steam. Have a towel on hand. Open the lid.
3. While macaroni is pressure cooking, in a medium-sized mixing bowl, beat 2 large eggs and mix in 1 tsp. ground mustard, 1 tsp. Sriracha and evaporated milk. Mix together well
4. On Instant Pot: use the Keep Warm function. Place unsalted butter in the cooked macaroni. Mix together well with silicone spatula and allow the butter to melt.
5. Pour in wet ingredients mixture and mix together well. Add grated cheese [⅓ portion at a time] and stir constantly until cheese is fully melted
6. If macaroni and cheese is too runny use the Sauté Less function - Click cancel, Sauté and Adjust button twice to reduce it down. Taste and season with kosher salt and ground black pepper. Serve.

Baked Chicken

[Servings: 8]

Ingredients:

- 8 Chicken Legs
- ¼ tsp. Five Spice Powder
- 2 tsp. Dried Sand Ginger
- 1 ¼ tsp. Kosher Salt
- Dash of Ground White Pepper [Optional]

Directions:

1. Place chicken legs in a large-sized mixing bowl. Pour in dried sand ginger, kosher salt and five spice powder. Mix together well. Place seasoned chicken legs on a large-sized piece of parchment paper [Do not use aluminum foil]. Wrap it up tightly and place it on a shallow dish with opening side facing upwards. Do not stack more than 2 levels of chicken legs
2. Place steamer rack in your Instant Pot and pour in 1 cup water. Carefully place chicken legs dish onto rack. Close the lid and cook at High pressure for approximately 18 to 26 minutes. Natural release for approximately 20 minutes [turn off heat and don't touch it]
3. Open lid carefully. Remove the dish from your Instant Pot and unwrap parchment paper carefully. Pour out all the juice into a small bowl, then place chicken legs on a wire rack on top of an oven tray. Put it under broiler until skin is browned but not dried out
4. The remaining meat juice can be used as the dipping sauce for chicken. Taste and add more dried sand ginger to desired liking. Serve.

Savory Mushroom Thyme Oatmeal

[Servings: 4]

Ingredients:

- 1 cup Steel Cut Oats
- 14-ounce can of Chicken Broth
- ½ cup Water
- ½ cup Smoked Gouda [Finely Grated]
- ½ Finely Diced Medium Onion
- 2 tbsp. Butter
- 2 cloves of Minced Garlic
- 8 ounces of Sliced Crimini Mushrooms
- 3 sprigs of Fresh Thyme [Additional for Garnish]
- Ground Pepper [For Seasoning]
- ¼ tsp. Salt
- 2 tbsp. Olive Oil
- Salt [For Seasoning]

Directions:

1. Add butter to Instant Pot. Select Sauté. When butter is melted, add onions and cook, stirring frequently, approximately 3 minutes until softened. Add garlic and cook for approximately 1 minute. Add oats and sauté for about 1 minute
2. Add broth, thyme, water and salt. Lock the lid in place. Select High pressure and cook for approximately 10 minutes. While oats are cooking, heat a large sauté pan over a medium-high heat until hot. Add olive oil and mushrooms and cook until they are golden brown on both sides
3. When the beep sounds, turn off your Instant Pot and use a Natural pressure release for approximately 10 minutes, then do a Quick pressure release to release any of the remaining pressure. When the valve drops carefully remove lid.
4. Stir oats. Stir in the Gouda until melted. Stir in mushrooms. Season with additional salt and ground pepper. Garnish with thyme leaves. Serve.

Beef Brisket

[Servings: 6]

Ingredients:

- 3 lbs. of Beef Brisket [Flat Cut and Fat Trimmed]
- 1 cup BBQ Sauce
- ½ cup Water
- 1 tbsp. Worcester Sauce
- 2 tbsp. Liquid Smoke
- ¼ tsp. Celery Salt
- ¼ tsp. Garlic Salt
- ¼ tsp. Lowry's Seasoned Salt
- 1 tsp. Seasoned Meat Tenderizer

Directions:

1. Combine meat tenderizer, celery salt, seasoned salt and garlic salt in a small-sized bowl. Rub spices into brisket. Put the brisket in a large-sized heavy duty Ziploc bag. Add liquid smoke and Worcester sauce. Seal bag and put in the refrigerator to marinate overnight
2. Put water and BBQ sauce in Instant Pot. Add brisket and any juices in the Ziploc bag. Select High pressure and set the timer for approximately 60 minutes
3. When the beep sounds, turn off your Instant Pot and let the pressure release naturally for about 15 minutes. Quick release any of the remaining pressure.
4. When the valve drops carefully remove the lid. Carefully remove meat from the Instant Pot to a large-sized platter and slice the meat across the grain. Add some additional BBQ sauce mixed with some of cooking liquid. Serve.

Cinnamon Roll Steel Cut Oats

[Servings: 4]

Ingredients:

- 1 cup Steel Cut Oats
- ¾ cup Raisins
- 3 ½ cups of Water
- 1 tbsp. Butter
- ¼ tsp. Salt

Brown Sugar Topping:

- 1 tsp. Cinnamon
- ¼ cup Packed Light Brown Sugar

Cream Cheese Topping:

- 2 ounces of Cream Cheese [Softened]
- 2 tbsp. Powdered Sugar
- 1 tsp. Milk

Directions:

1. Add butter to your Instant Pot and select Sauté. When butter is melted add oats and toast, stirring constantly, until they begin to darken and smell nutty. Should take approximately 3 minutes
2. Add water and salt to Instant Pot. Select High pressure and set for a 10-minute cook time. When the beep sounds, turn off your Instant Pot and use a Natural pressure release for approximately 5 minutes and then do Quick pressure release to release any of the remaining pressure
3. When the valve drops carefully remove lid. Stir oats. Stir in raisins. Cover and allow to sit for 10 minutes until oats are the desired thickness.
4. In a small-sized bowl, mix together brown sugar and cinnamon. Set to the side.
5. In a small-sized bowl, whisk together cream cheese, milk and powder sugar. Add more milk or powdered sugar as necessary to make an icing that will swirl. Place in individual bowls topped with brown sugar topping and a swirl of cream cheese topping. Serve.

Apple Sauce

[**Servings:** 6]

Ingredients:

- 10 cups of Peeled and Diced Apple
- ½ cup Sugar
- 1 cup Water
- 1 tsp. Cinnamon

Directions:

1. Place all of ingredients in Instant Pot. Lock the lid into place and seal the steam nozzle. Cook on Manual for approximately 8 minutes. Quick release the pressure
2. Remove lid and blend to desired consistency using either an immersion blender or traditional blender. Blend in batches. Serve.

Breakfast Quinoa

[**Servings:** 6]

Ingredients:

- 1 ½ cups of Uncooked Quinoa [Rinsed]
- 2 ¼ cups of Water
- 2 tbsp. Maple Syrup
- ½ tsp. Vanilla
- ¼ tsp. Ground Cinnamon
- Pinch of Salt

Optional Toppings:

- Sliced Almonds
- Fresh berries
- Milk

Directions:

1. Add quinoa, vanilla, water, cinnamon, maple syrup and salt to Instant Pot. Select High pressure and set cook time for approximately 1 minute. When the beep sounds turn your Instant Pot off, wait about 10 minutes and then use Quick pressure release to release any of the remaining pressure.
2. When valve drops carefully remove the lid, tilting away from you to allow any steam to safely disperse. Fluff quinoa and add any optional toppings if desired. Serve

Crust less Quiche

[**Servings:** 4]

Ingredients:

- 6 Large Eggs [Well Beaten]
- 4 slices of Bacon [Cooked and Crumbled]
- 2 Large Chopped Green Onions
- 1 cup Shredded Cheese
- 1 ½ cups of Water
- 1 cup Cooked Ground Sausage
- ½ cup Milk
- ½ cup Diced Ham
- ¼ tsp. Salt
- 1/8 tsp. Ground Black Pepper

Directions:

1. Put metal trivet in the bottom of your Instant Pot and add 1 ½ cups of water. In a large-sized bowl whisk together eggs, salt, milk and pepper. Add ham, bacon, sausage, cheese and green onions to a 1-quart souffle dish and mix together well. Pour egg mixture over top of meat and stir together well to combine
2. Loosely cover souffle dish with aluminum foil. Use an aluminum foil sling to place dish on trivet in the Instant Pot. Lock the lid in place. Select High pressure and cook for approximately 30 minutes. When the timer beeps, turn off and wait 10 minutes before using the Quick pressure release

3. Carefully open lid and lift out the dish. Remove the foil. If you desire, sprinkle the top of quiche with some additional cheese and broil until melted and lightly browned. Serve

Chicken Walking Tacos

[Servings: 8]

Ingredients:

- 2 Large Boneless Skinless Chicken Breasts
- 1 can of Black Beans [Drained and Rinsed]
- 1 (1/4-ounce) package of Taco Seasoning Mix
- 1 cup Chunky Salsa
- 1 cup Water
- Fritos or Tortilla Chips

Toppings:

- Diced Tomatoes
- Diced Avocados
- Sour Cream
- Shredded Lettuce
- Shredded Mexican Cheese

Directions:

1. Add water, salsa and taco seasoning mix to Instant Pot. Stir well to combine. Add chicken breasts.
2. Cover and lock the lid in place. Select High pressure and set 4 minutes' cook time. When the timer beeps, turn off your Instant Pot and use a Quick pressure release. Use a slotted spoon to remove chicken to a cutting board and cut into small bite size pieces
3. Add chicken and black beans to Instant Pot. Select Sauté and cook, stirring often, until most of water has evaporated. Open bag of Frito chips and crush slightly. Top crushed chips with a scoop of hot taco meat and choice of toppings. Serve.

Cream and Berries Breakfast Cake

[Servings: 6]

Ingredients:

Breakfast Cake:

- 5 Eggs
- ¾ cup Ricotta Cheese
- ¾ cup Plain or Vanilla Yogurt
- 1 cup Whole Wheat Pastry Flour
- ½ cup Berry Compote [Your Desired Preference]
- ¼ cup Sugar
- 2 tsp. Vanilla Extract
- 2 tsp. Baking Powder
- 2 tbsp. Melted Butter
- ½ tsp. Salt

Sweet Yogurt Glaze:

- ¼ cup Yogurt
- 2 tbsp. Powdered Sugar
- ½ tsp. Vanilla Extract
- 1 tsp. Milk

Directions:

1. Make sure berry compote is cold and thick. If used warm, it has a tendency to sink to the bottom of pan.

Breakfast Cake:

2. Generously grease 6-cup bundt pan with a nonstick cooking spray. Beat together sugar and eggs until smooth. Add butter, yogurt, ricotta cheese and vanilla. Mix together until smooth
3. In a separate bowl, whisk together salt, flour and baking powder. Combine with egg mixture. Pour into greased bundt pan
4. Using a ½ cup berry compote, drop it by the tbsp. on top of batter and swirl in with knife.

5. Add 1 cup water to your Instant Pot and place trivet inside. Carefully place bundt pan on the trivet. Secure lid and turn the pressure release knob to a sealed position. Cook at High pressure for approximately 25 minutes

Sweet Yogurt Glaze:
1. While cake is cooking, whisk together milk, yogurt, vanilla and powdered sugar. Set to the side.
2. When cake is done being cooked in Instant Pot, use a Natural release for approximately 10 minutes and then release any of the remaining pressure.
3. Remove pan from the Instant Pot. Allow it to cool slightly. Loosen the sides of cake from pan and gently turn over onto plate. Drizzle with sweet yogurt glaze mixture. Serve

Almond Steel Cut Oats

[Servings: 4]

Ingredients:

- 1 cup Steel Cut Oats
- 3 ½ cups of Almond Coconut Milk
- ¼ cup Sliced Almonds
- ¼ cup Mini Chocolate Chips
- 1 tbsp. Butter
- ¼ cup Toasted Shredded Coconut
- ¼ tsp. Salt

Directions:

1. Add butter to your Instant Pot and select Sauté. When butter is melted add oats and toast, stirring constantly, until they smell nutty. Should take about 3 minutes. Add milk and salt. Select High pressure and set for approximately 10 minutes
2. When the beep sounds, turn off your Instant Pot and use a Natural pressure release for approximately 10 minutes and then do a Quick pressure release to release any of the remaining pressure. When the valve drops carefully remove lid.
3. Stir oats. Cover and allow to sit for 5 minutes until the oats are desired thickness. Top with shredded coconut, sliced almonds, chocolate chips and a splash of milk. Serve.

Eggs de Provence

[Servings: 6]

Ingredients:

- 6 Eggs
- 1 cup Chopped Kale Leaves
- 1 cup Cooked Ham
- 1 cup Cheddar Cheese
- ½ cup Heavy Cream
- 1 Chopped Onion
- 1 tbsp. Herbs de Provence
- ½ tbsp. Salt
- ½ tbsp. Pepper

Directions:

1. Whisk eggs with heavy cream. Put in the rest of ingredients and mix together well. Put mixture in heatproof dish and cover it.
2. Put 1 cup water inside Instant Pot, then trivet and then eggs. Set your Instant Pot on Manual with High pressure for approximately 20 minutes with a Natural pressure release. Remove from your Instant Pot once finished. Serve

Crust less Tomato Spinach Quiche

[**Servings:** 6]

Ingredients:

- 12 Large Eggs
- 3 Large Sliced Green Onions
- 1 cup Diced Seeded Tomato
- ¼ cup Shredded Parmesan Cheese
- 3 cups of Fresh Baby Spinach [Roughly Chopped]
- 1 ½ cups of Water
- ½ cup Milk
- 4 Tomato Slices
- ½ tsp. Salt
- ¼ tsp. Fresh Ground Black Pepper

Directions:

1. Put trivet in the bottom of your Instant Pot and add 1 ½ cups of water. In a large-sized bowl whisk together milk, eggs, pepper and salt. Add tomato, spinach and green onions to a 1 ½ quart baking dish and mix together well.
2. Pour egg mixture over veggies and stir well to combine. Gently place sliced tomatoes on top and sprinkle with Parmesan cheese.
3. Use a sling to place dish on the trivet in Instant Pot. Lock the lid in place. Select High Pressure and cook for approximately 20 minutes
4. When the timer beeps, turn off, wait about 10 minutes, then use the quick Pressure release. Carefully open lid, lift out dish and if desired broil until lightly browned. Serve.

Sausage and Peppers

[**Servings:** 5]

Ingredients:

- 4 Large Green Bell Peppers [Seeded, Cored, and Cut into 1/2-Inch Strips]
- 2 (19-ounce) packages of Johnsonville Italian Sausage [10 sausages]
- 28-ounce can of Diced Tomatoes
- 15-ounce can of Tomato Sauce
- 1 tbsp. Basil
- 1 cup Water
- 1 tbsp. Italian Seasoning
- 2 tsp. Garlic Powder

Directions:

1. In Instant Pot, combine tomatoes, water, tomato sauce, basil, garlic powder and Italian seasoning. Add sausages to sauce.
2. Place peppers on top of sausage, but don't mix together. Lock lid in place and select High pressure. Set timer for approximately 25 minutes and press start
3. When the beep sounds turn off your Instant Pot and use a Quick pressure release to release any remaining pressure. When the valve drops carefully remove lid. Serve

Cherry Apple Risotto

[**Servings:** 2]

Ingredients:

- 2 Large Apples [Cored and Diced]
- 1 cup Apple Juice
- ½ cup Dried Cherries
- 1 ½ cups of Arborio Rice
- ⅓ cup Brown Sugar
- 3 cups of 1% Milk
- ¼ tsp. Salt
- 1 ½ tsp. Cinnamon
- 2 tbsp. Butter

Optional Toppings:

- Brown Sugar
- Sliced Almonds
- 1% Milk

Directions:

1. Heat butter in your Instant Pot for approximately 2 to 3 minutes. Stir in rice and cook, stirring frequently, until rice becomes opaque. Should take approximately 3 to 4 minutes
2. Add apples, spices and brown sugar. Stir in juice and milk. Select High pressure and cook for approximately 6 minutes. After 6 minutes, turn off your Instant Pot and use a Quick pressure release. Carefully remove the lid and stir in dried cherries. Top with sliced almonds, additional brown sugar and a splash of milk. Serve.

Steel Cut Oats

[**Servings:** 2]

Ingredients:

- ½ cup Steel Cut Oats
- 2 cups of Water
- 1 tbsp. Oil
- Dash of Salt

Optional Toppings:

- Sweetener
- Milk
- Fruit
- Chopped Nuts

Directions:

1. Combine ingredients in Instant Pot, select High pressure and cook for approximately 10 minutes. When the beep sounds, turn off your Instant Pot and use a Natural pressure release for approximately 10 minutes and then do a Quick pressure release to release any of the remaining pressure
2. When the valve drops carefully remove the lid. Stir oats and allow to sit for a minute to absorb the water. Top with milk, fruit, chopped nuts and favorite sweetener. Serve.

Carrot Cake Oatmeal

[**Servings:** 6]

Ingredients:

- 1 cup Steel Cut Oats
- ¼ cup Chia Seeds
- 1 cup Grated Carrots
- ¾ cup Raisins
- 4 cups of Water
- 1 tbsp. Butter
- 3 tbsp. Maple Syrup
- 2 tsp. Cinnamon
- 1 tsp. Pumpkin Pie Spice
- ¼ tsp. Salt

Optional Toppings:

- Maple Syrup
- Milk
- Raisins
- Chopped Nuts

Directions:

1. Add butter to the Instant Pot and select Sauté. When butter is melted add oats and toast, stirring constantly, until they smell nutty. Should take approximately 3 minutes
2. Add water, cinnamon, carrots, salt, maple syrup and pumpkin pie spice. Select High pressure and cook for approximately 10 minutes.
3. When the beep sounds, turn off your Instant Pot and use a Natural pressure release for about 10 minutes and then do a Quick pressure release to release any of remaining pressure. When the valve drops carefully remove lid.
4. Stir oats. Stir in raisins and chia seeds. Cover and allow to sit for 5 to 10 minutes until oats are the desired thickness. Top with additional raisins, chopped nuts, maple syrup and milk. Serve.

Chicken Tacos

[**Servings:** 12]

Ingredients:

- 3 lbs. of Quartered Chicken Boneless Breasts
- 24 individual Corn Tortillas
- 1 Dried Ancho Chile
- 3 cups of Tomato Puree
- 1 ¼ cups of Diced Onion
- 1 cup Hot Water
- ½ tsp. Chipotle Powder
- 4 tsp. Minced Garlic Cloves
- 1 tbsp. Cumin
- 1 tsp. Sea Salt

Directions:

1. Place Ancho chile in bowl and pour boiling water over it. Allow to soak for approximately 5 to 10 minutes. Place chile and soaking water into a blender with garlic, cumin, chipotle powder and sea salt. Blend on high until pureed.
2. Place pureed mixture into Instant Pot. Top with chicken, onions and tomato puree. Lock the lid into place and seal the steam nozzle
3. Cook on the Poultry setting or manual for approximately 15 minutes. Natural release for approximately 5 minutes then Quick release any of the remaining pressure. After chicken is done, use two forks to shred chicken. Spoon taco filling into tortillas. Serve.

Strawberries Steel Cut Oats

[Servings: 4]

Ingredients:

- 1 cup Steel Cut Oats
- 1 ½ cups of Sliced Strawberries
- ¼ cup Cream
- ¼ cup Chia Seeds
- 4 cups of Water
- 3 tbsp. Light Brown Sugar
- 1 tbsp. Butter
- ¼ tsp. Salt

Optional Toppings:

- Sliced Strawberries
- Brown Sugar
- Sliced Almonds
- Cream

Directions:

1. Add butter to your Instant Pot and select Sauté. When butter is melted add oats and toast, stirring constantly, until they smell nutty. Should take approximately 3 minutes. Add water, brown sugar, cream and salt. Select High pressure and cook for 10 minutes.
2. When the beep sounds, turn off your Instant Pot and use a Natural pressure release for approximately 10 minutes and then do a Quick pressure release to release any of the remaining pressure. When the valve drops carefully remove lid
3. Stir oats. Stir in strawberries and chia seeds. Cover and allow to sit for 5 to 10 minutes until oats are desired thickness. Top with additional sliced strawberries, sliced almonds, brown sugar and a splash of cream. Serve.

Buffalo Chicken

[Servings: 8]

Ingredients:

- 3 lbs. Of Quartered Chicken Boneless Breasts
- 1 ounce of Ranch Dressing Mix
- 12 fluid ounces of Buffalo Wing Sauce

Directions:

1. Place chicken, buffalo sauce and ranch dressing mix in Instant Pot. Lock the cover into place and seal the steam nozzle. Select the Poultry setting or set manually for approximately 15 minutes
2. Naturally release pressure for about 5 minutes then Quick release the remaining pressure. Shred chicken with fork and add sauce to the side. Serve.

Apple Steel Cut Oats

[Servings: 4]

Ingredients:

- 1 cup Steel Cut Oats
- 1 Large Apple [Peeled; Cored, and Diced]
- 3 ½ cups of Water
- 1 tbsp. Butter
- 1 ½ tsp. Ground Cinnamon
- ¼ tsp. Salt
- 2 tbsp. Light Brown Sugar

Optional Toppings:

- Nuts
- Brown Sugar
- Milk

Directions:

1. Add butter to your Instant Pot and select Sauté. When butter is melted add oats and toast, stirring constantly, until they start to darken and smell nutty. Should take approximately 3 minutes. Add water, cinnamon, apples, salt and brown sugar. Select High pressure and cook for approximately 10 minutes
2. When the beep sounds, turn off your Instant Pot and use a Natural pressure release for approximately 10 minutes and then do a Quick pressure release to release any of the remaining pressure.
3. When the valve drops carefully remove lid. Stir the oats. Cover and allow to sit for 5 to 10 minutes until oats are the desired thickness. Top with nuts, milk and additional brown sugar if you desire. Serve.

Cranberry Bake French Toast

[**Servings:** 8]

Ingredients:

Cranberry Orange Sauce:

- 2 cups of Fresh Cranberries [Washed]
- ¼ cup Fresh Orange Juice
- ½ cup Granulated Sugar
- ¼ tsp. Ground Cinnamon
- ¼ tsp. Salt

French Toast:

- 1 Orange [Finely Grated Zest]
- 1 loaf of Challah Bread [Cubed]
- 2 cups of Whole Milk
- 3 Eggs [Beaten]
- ½ cup Sugar
- 4 tbsp. Melted Butter
- 1 tsp. Vanilla Extract
- ¼ tsp. Salt

Directions:

1. Bring cranberries, ½ cup sugar, orange juice, ¼ tsp. cinnamon and ¼ tsp. salt to a boil in saucepan over a medium-high heat. Cook until berries have popped and thickened slightly about 5 minutes. Remove from the heat. Pour into a buttered 7x3-inch cake pan, or similar glass or metal baking dish. [Make sure it fits inside Instant Pot.]
2. In a large-sized bowl, whisk together ½ cup sugar and melted butter. Add milk, orange zest, beaten eggs, vanilla and salt. Mix in cubed bread. Allow it to rest until bread absorbs the milk, stirring it occasionally.
3. Spread bread mixture on top of cranberry sauce in the pan. Prepare a foil sling for lifting dish out of your Instant Pot by taking an 18-inch strip of foil and folding it lengthwise twice
4. Pour 1 cup water into your Instant Pot and place trivet in the bottom. Center pan on foil strip and lower it into Instant Pot.
5. Lock lid in place. Select High Pressure and set timer for approximately 25 minutes. When the beep sounds, turn off your Instant Pot and do a Quick pressure release to release all the pressure. When valve drops carefully remove the lid. Remove dish from Instant Pot. If desired, place dish under broiler to brown up the top. Serve.

Lunch Recipes

Root Beer Pull Pork Sandwiches

[Servings: 4]

Ingredients:

- 2 lbs. of Quartered Pork Roast
- 1 ¼ cups of Sliced Onion
- ¾ cup Root Beer
- ¼ cup Ketchup
- 4 Sandwich Rolls
- ½ tbsp. Lemon Juice
- 1 tbsp. All-Purpose Flour
- 1 tbsp. Honey
- 2 tbsp. Tomato Paste
- 1 tbsp. Worcestershire Sauce
- ½ tsp. Garlic Salt
- ½ tsp. Black Pepper

Directions:

1. Sprinkle roast with garlic salt and pepper. Place in Instant Pot. Mix all of other ingredients together and pour over roast. Lock cover into place and seal the steam nozzle.
2. Select the Meat / Stew option or Manual for approximately 35 minutes. Naturally release the pressure for about 5 minutes then Quick release the remaining pressure. Remove roast and onions. Shred the pork and discard the onions
3. Add roast back to sauce in the pot and stir well to combine. Place ¼ of pulled pork into each of 4 rolls. Serve.

Chicken Lettuce Wraps

[Servings: 4]

Ingredients:

- 1 lb. of Ground Chicken
- 8 leaves of Romaine Lettuce
- ½ cup Drained Sliced Water Chestnuts [Canned]
- ¼ cup Chicken Broth
- ¼ cup Coconut Aminos
- ⅓ cup Green Onion [Scallion]
- ¾ cup Diced Onion
- 5 tsp. Minced Garlic Cloves
- 1/8 tsp. Ground Allspice
- ½ tsp. Ground Ginger
- 2 tbsp. Balsamic Vinegar

Directions:

1. Place all ingredients except for the lettuce in Instant Pot. Lock the lid into place and seal the steam nozzle. Cook on the Manual setting for approximately 10 minutes.
2. Quick release the pressure. Use fork or meat masher to break up the chunks of meat. Spoon meat into lettuce leaves and sprinkle with green onions. Serve.

Chicken Tinga

[Servings: 6]

Ingredients:

- 3 Large Diced Uncooked Chicken Breasts
- 15-ounce can of Fire-Roasted Diced Tomatoes [With Liquid]
- 15-ounce can of Black or Pinto Beans [Drained and Rinsed]
- 1 Large Diced Tomatillo
- 4 ounces of Grated Cheddar Cheese
- 2 Minced Chipotle Chiles in Adobo Sauce
- 1/2 Diced Large Sweet Onion
- 1 tbsp. Vegetable Oil
- 2 cloves of Minced Garlic
- 1 tsp. Ground Cumin
- 1 tsp. Dried Mexican Oregano
- 1 tbsp. Cayenne Pepper Sauce
- ¼ cup Water
- 6 12-Inch Flour Tortillas
- 1 tsp. Salt

Directions:

1. Preheat Instant Pot. Add oil and onion and cook until softened, should take about 3 minutes. Add garlic and cook for approximately 1 minute. Add tomatillo, cumin, oregano and salt and cook, stirring constantly, another 3 minutes. Add tomatoes, chipotles, water and cayenne pepper sauce. Puree mixture until it's very smooth.
2. Stir in chicken. Select High pressure and set 4 minute cook time. When the timer beeps, turn your Instant Pot off and do a Quick pressure release
3. Select Sauté and cook, stirring occasionally and gently, until sauce clings to chicken and most of liquid has evaporated. Mash beans with a potato masher or fork, until chunky. Assemble burritos by spooning chicken mixture onto tortillas. Add beans and sprinkle with cheese. Roll burritos as desired. Serve.

Teriyaki Chicken Wings

[Servings: 4-6]

Ingredients:

- 3 lbs. of Chicken Wings [Drum and Wings Separated]
- 1 cup Low Sodium Teriyaki Sauce
- 1 tbsp. Lemon Juice
- 6 tbsp. Sesame Oil
- 2 tbsp. Sugar
- ½ tsp. Crushed Red Pepper
- Toasted Sesame Seeds [For Garnish]

Directions:

1. Combine chicken wings, 4 tbsp. sesame oil, Teriyaki sauce, lemon juice and sugar in a large-sized bowl or Zip Lock bag. Refrigerate for at least 2 hours or overnight to marinate. Select Browning and add 2 tbsp. sesame oil to Instant Pot. When oil is hot, using tongs, remove chicken wings from marinade [reserving marinade] and place wings in your Instant Pot to brown. Stir around, lightly browning wings on all sides
2. Pour marinade over browned wings. Lock the lid in place, select High pressure and set the timer for 7 minutes cooking time
3. When the beep sounds, turn off your Instant Pot and use a Natural pressure release for 10 minutes, then do a Quick pressure release to release any of the remaining pressure. When the valve drops carefully remove lid.
4. With tongs, remove wings and place on a cookie sheet and place in oven under a broiler or 400 degrees until crispy. Should take 6 to 8 minutes. Garnish with toasted sesame seeds and crushed red pepper. Serve

Cola Chicken Wings

[**Servings:** 4]

Ingredients:

- 1 ½ lb. of Chicken Wings
- 200 ml of Coca-Cola
- 1 stalk of Green Onion [Cut 2-Inches Long]
- 4 cloves of Crushed Garlic
- 1 tbsp. Dark Soy Sauce
- 1 tbsp. Peanut Oil
- 1 tbsp. Chinese Rice Wine
- 1 tbsp. Sliced Ginger
- 2 tbsp. Light Soy Sauce

Directions:

1. Press Sauté button on Instant Pot. Wait until indicator says "Hot". Pour in 1 tbsp. peanut oil into Instant Pot. Ensure to coat the oil over the whole bottom of pot. Add crushed garlic, sliced ginger and green onions into the pot, then stir for approximately 1 minute until fragrant.
2. Add chicken wings into the pot and stir fry them together with garlic, ginger slices and green onions for approximately 1 to 2 minutes
3. When the edges of the chicken skin begin to brown, pour in Coca-Cola and fully deglaze the bottom of pot with a wooden spoon. Add in light soy sauce, dark soy sauce, Chinese rice wine. Mix together well.
4. Close the lid and pressure cook at High pressure for approximately 5 minutes. Turn off the heat and Natural release for about 10 minutes. Open lid carefully and taste one of chicken wings and cola sauce [It shouldn't taste like Coca-Cola]. Reduce and season sauce with more salt if so desired. Serve

Cheesy Noodles

[**Servings:** 8]

Ingredients:

- 2 Bouillon Beef Cubes
- 8 ounces of Shredded Cheddar Cheese
- 16 ounces of Cooked Egg Noodles
- 32 ounces of Diced Tomatoes [Canned]
- 3 cups of Cooked Ground Beef
- 3 cups of Sliced Green Bell Pepper
- 1 cup Diced Onion
- 2 tbsp. Cornstarch
- 4 tbsp. Water
- 4 tbsp. Soy Sauce [Low Sodium]
- ¼ tsp. Garlic Powder
- 2 tsp. Sugar

Directions:

1. Combine ground beef, tomatoes, onions, garlic powder, beef bouillon cubes and water in Instant Pot. Cook on the Manual setting for approximately 10 minutes. Quick release the pressure
2. Add in soy sauce, sugar, cornstarch and green peppers. Sauté for approximately 5 minutes. Cook noodles according to package directions. Combine noodles and cheddar cheese. Add mixture over cheesy noodles. Serve.

Tex Mex Chili Mac

[Servings: 4]

Ingredients:

- 1 lb. of Lean Ground Sausage
- 1 cup Frozen Corn
- 2 cups of Elbow Macaroni
- 2 cups of Water
- 1 Diced Yellow Onion
- 3 cloves of Minced Garlic
- 7-ounce can of Green Chiles
- 15-ounce of Tomato Sauce
- 1 tbsp. Chili Powder
- 2 tbsp. Minced Fresh Cilantro
- 1 tbsp. Vegetable Oil
- ¼ tsp. Cayenne Pepper
- 1 tsp. Salt

Directions:

1. Put oil in your Instant Pot and select Browning. When oil begins to sizzle, sauté beef, onion and garlic until meat is no longer pink and onion is tender. Should take about 10 minutes. Transfer to bowl lined with paper towels to remove any excess fat.
2. Add beef, macaroni, water, green chiles, tomato sauce, cayenne pepper, chili powder and salt to Instant Pot and stir well to combine
3. Select High pressure. Set timer for 5 minutes and press start. When the beep sounds turn your Instant Pot off and use a Quick pressure release. When the valve drops carefully remove lid
4. Stir in frozen corn. Select Sauté and cook until corn is heated and the macaroni is tender. Stir in cilantro. Top with sour cream, shredded Mexican cheese and tortilla chips. Serve.

Barbeque Bacon Apple Chicken

[Servings: 4]

Ingredients:

- 2 lbs. of Quartered Chicken Boneless Breasts
- 8 ounces of Tomato Paste
- 8 pieces of Bacon
- 4 cups of Diced Apple
- 1 ¼ cups of Diced Onion
- 3 tbsp. Molasses
- 1 tbsp. Dijon Mustard
- 1 tbsp. Apple Cider Vinegar
- 1 tbsp. Maple Syrup
- 2 tbsp. Coconut Aminos
- 2 tsp. Minced Garlic Cloves
- 2 tsp. Smoked Paprika
- ½ tsp. Sea Salt

Directions:

1. In bowl, combine molasses, tomato paste, garlic, maple syrup, apple cider vinegar, smoked paprika, coconut aminos, garlic, sea salt and Dijon mustard. Stir in diced apple and onion. Wrap bacon slices around the chicken breasts and place in Instant Pot. Top with BBQ mixture
2. Lock lid in place and seal the steam nozzle. Cook on Manual for approximately 10 minutes. Natural release for about 5 minutes then Quick release any of the remaining pressure. Remove chicken breast and add the BBQ sauce on the side. Serve.

Santa Fe Chicken

[Servings: 8]

Ingredients:

- 1 lb. of Quartered Chicken Boneless Breasts
- 15 ½ ounces of Drained and Rinsed Black Beans [Canned]
- 10 ounces of Diced Tomatoes with Green Chiles
- 10 fluid ounces of Chicken Broth
- 1 cup Frozen Corn
- 4 cups of Corn Chips
- ⅓ cups of Dice Green Onion [Scallion]
- 1 tsp. Onion Powder
- 1 tsp. Garlic Powder
- 1 tsp. Cumin
- 1 tsp. Dried Cilantro
- 1 tsp. Cayenne Pepper
- 1/8 tsp. Salt

Directions:

1. In Instant Pot, combine chicken broth, beans, tomatoes, onions, corn and seasonings. Place chicken breasts on top. Lock lid into place and seal the steam nozzle
2. Select the Poultry button and cook for approximately 10 minutes. Natural release for about 5 minutes then Quick release any of the remaining pressure. Remove chicken and shred. Return to your Instant Pot and stir well to combine. Add corn tortilla chips. Serve.

Wheat Berry Salad

[Servings: 4]

Ingredients:

- ¾ cup Dried Blueberries
- ¾ cup Thinly Sliced Green Onions
- ½ cup Slivered Dried Apricots
- ½ cup Chopped Toasted Almonds
- 2 cups of Water
- ¼ cup Raspberry Vinegar
- 1 cup Wheat Berries
- 2 tsp. Dijon Mustard
- 1 tbsp. Balsamic Vinegar
- 3 tbsp. Oil
- 2 tbsp. Chopped Fresh Parsley
- ¾ tsp. Salt
- ½ tsp. Pepper

Directions:

1. Rinse wheat berries well with cold water and place them in a bowl filled with cold water. Soak them over night. Rinse thoroughly and drain them
2. Place wheat berries in your Instant Pot with 2 cups of water and pressure cook for approximately 15 to 20 minutes, manually release the pressure when done. Rinse with cold water and drain
3. Whisk together raspberry vinegar, balsamic vinegar, mustard, salt and pepper in bowl. Gradually whisk in oil until blended. Stir in apricots, onions, almonds, blueberries and parsley
4. Allow it to stand for approximately 30 minutes. Stir in wheat berries. Cover and refrigerate for 4 hours. Garnish with fresh parsley. Serve.

Chicken Cacciatore

[**Servings:** 4-6]

Ingredients:

- 2 lbs. of Boneless Skinless Chicken Thighs
- ¼ cup Low Sodium Chicken Broth
- 28-ounce can of Diced Tomatoes
- 2 Green Bell Peppers [Cut into 1-Inch Squares]
- 1 Large Minced Onion
- 3 cloves of Minced Garlic
- 1 Bay Leaf
- 2 tbsp. Extra-Virgin Olive Oil
- ¼ tsp. Red Pepper Flakes
- 1 tsp. Dried Oregano
- Pepper
- Salt

Directions:

1. Heat olive oil in your Instant Pot using the Browning setting. Sprinkle chicken with salt and pepper. Working in batches cook chicken until golden brown. Should take about 5 minutes total, adding more oil as necessary. Transfer chicken to a plate
2. Add onion to Instant Pot. Sauté until onion is soft, scraping up any browned bits. Should take about 4 minutes. Add garlic, oregano and red pepper flakes and cook until fragrant. Should take about 1 minute.
3. Add bay leaf, tomatoes and chicken broth. Return chicken to your Instant Pot and press into tomatoes until they are mostly covered.
4. Place lid on your Instant Pot and lock in place. Cook on High pressure for approximately 10 minutes. Release pressure using Quick release valve and remove lid. Add green peppers and stir into mixture
5. Lock lid in place again, bring to High pressure and cook for 2 more minutes. Use the Quick release and remove lid. Remove bay leaf. Season to taste with salt and pepper. Add some rice or pasta if you so desire. Serve.

Chicken Marsala

[**Servings:** 4]

Ingredients:

- 3 lbs. of Boneless Skinless Chicken Thighs [Well Trimmed]
- 8 ounces Sliced Mushrooms
- 4 slices of Diced Peppered Bacon
- 1 cup Chicken Broth
- ½ cup Sweet Marsala Wine
- 2 tbsp. Chopped Parsley
- 3 tbsp. Cold Water
- 3 tbsp. Butter [Divided]
- 1 tbsp. Vegetable Oil
- 2 tbsp. Cornstarch
- Salt
- Pepper
- Chopped Parsley [For Garnish]

Directions:

1. Select Browning and add diced bacon to Instant Pot. Brown bacon until crisp, stirring frequently. Remove bacon to a plate, leaving bacon fat in the pot. Season chicken with salt and pepper. Add chicken to the pot and brown on both sides in bacon fat. Cook chicken in batches. Remove chicken to a platter, leaving the fat in pan.
2. Add marsala to deglaze pot and allow it to almost completely evaporate to concentrate the flavor and remove most of liquid
3. Add chicken broth and browned chicken to Instant Pot, along with any juices that have collected on platter. Cover the pot and lock the lid in place.
4. Select High pressure and set the timer for 10 minutes' cook time. [It will take about 10 minutes to reach high pressure
5. While chicken is cooking, heat a large sauté pan over a medium-high heat until hot. Add oil and 1 tbsp. butter. When butter is melted, add the mushrooms and cook until golden. Season with salt and pepper.

When the timer beeps, do a Quick pressure release and remove chicken from the Instant Pot to a serving dish.
6. Combine cornstarch and water, whisking until smooth. Add cornstarch mixture to the sauce in the pot stirring constantly. Select Simmer and bring to a boil, stirring constantly. Stir in remaining 2 tbsp. butter. Add mushrooms and stir to coat with sauce
7. Adjust seasoning if desired. Combine sauce with chicken in serving bowl. Serve topped with crumbled bacon and chopped parsley. Serve.

Barbeque Chicken Strip Salad

[Servings: 4]

Ingredients:

- 1 lb. of Frozen Chicken Breasts
- ½ cup Ketchup
- ⅓ cup Water
- Dash of Red Pepper Flakes
- ¾ tsp. McCormick's BBQ Seasoning
- ¼ tsp. Dried Italian Seasoning
- 2 tsp. Honey

Optional Fixings:

- Walnuts
- Flax Seeds
- Shredded Cheeses
- Lettuce
- Spinach
- Tomatoes
- Pine Nuts
- Salad Dressing [Your Choice]

Directions:

1. Spray the bottom of your Instant Pot with nonstick spray. Place frozen chicken breasts and ⅓ cup water in pot and put the lid on. Press the steam button and set the time to approximately 8 minutes. The pot will come to pressure in about eight minutes and then cook for another eight minutes.
2. While the breasts are thawing in your Instant Pot prepare salad fixings using whatever optional fixings you desire and place them in into serving bowls
3. In a separate bowl, mix together ketchup, BBQ seasoning, red pepper flakes, Italian seasoning and honey.
4. When your Instant Pot beeps that it is finished, throw a dish towel over the top and do a Quick pressure release. Remove the top.
5. With chicken still in the pot, use a large fork and long sharp knife to slice chicken into ½ inch strips being careful to not touch the sides of pot. The chicken will be raw in the middle but easily sliceable. Pour the BBQ sauce over chicken and mix with a heat safe spoon
6. Press the Sauté button and set the time for approximately 18 minutes. This will come to a good boil. As the sauce thickens, for the last 5 minutes it is important that you stay with the pot and monitor the sauce.
7. Move the chicken around in the pot a little while the sauce thickens and sticks to the chicken. When almost all of sauce has stuck to the chicken, remove chicken to a serving tray.
8. Turn the pot off. Immediately pour 2 to 3 cups of water into your Instant Pot to keep the remaining sauce residue from sticking and burning pot. Lay BBQ chicken on top of the salads. Serve.

Indian Butter Chicken

[Servings: 8]

Ingredients:

- 10 Boneless Skinless Chicken Thighs
- 2 Jalapeno Peppers [Seeded and Chopped]
- 2 (14-ounce) cans of Diced Tomatoes and Juice
- ¾ cup Greek Yogurt
- ¼ cup Firmly Packed Minced Cilantro
- ¾ cup Heavy Cream
- ½ cup Unsalted Butter
- 2 tsp. Ground Cumin
- 2 tsp. Kosher Salt
- 2 tsp. Garam Masala
- 2 tsp. Ground Roasted Cumin Seeds
- 2 tbsp. Fresh Ginger Root [Peeled and Chopped]
- 2 tbsp. Water
- 2 tbsp. Cornstarch
- 1 tbsp. Paprika

Directions:

1. Cut chicken pieces into quarters. Put tomatoes, jalapeno and ginger in blender or food processor and blend to a fine puree. Add butter to Instant Pot, select Browning. When butter is melted and foam begins to subside, add chicken pieces, a few at a time and sear until they are nicely browned all over [about 2 to 3 minutes per batch]. Remove them with slotted spoon into a bowl and put to the side.
2. Add ground cumin and paprika to butter in the pot and cook, stirring rapidly, for 10 to 15 seconds. Add tomato mixture, salt, cream, yogurt and chicken pieces [with any juices that have accumulated in bowl] to the pot.
3. Gently stir chicken to coat the pieces. Cover and lock the lid in place. Select High pressure and set the timer for 5 minutes cook time. When the timer beeps, turn off and use a Natural pressure release for about 10 minutes. After approximately 10 minutes use a Quick pressure release to release any of the remaining pressure
4. Stir in garam masala and roasted cumin. Whisk together cornstarch and water in a small-sized bowl. Stir into sauce in pot. Select Sauté and bring to a boil. Turn off Instant Pot and stir in minced cilantro. Serve.

Chicken Parmesan Meatballs in Ranch Sauce

[Servings: 4]

Ingredients:

- 1 lb. of Ground Chicken
- 14-ounce can of Chicken Broth
- 2 ounces of Cream Cheese
- ⅓ cup Seasoned Breadcrumbs
- ⅓ cup Sour Cream
- ½ cup Freshly Grated Parmesan Cheese
- 1 tbsp. Chopped Parsley
- 1 clove of Minced Garlic
- 1 Large Egg [Beaten]
- 1 tbsp. Vegetable Oil
- 2 tbsp. Finely Chopped Onion
- 2 tbsp. Cornstarch
- 3 tbsp. Water
- 1 tsp. Lemon Juice
- 2 tsp. Ranch Dressing Seasoning Mix
- ¼ tsp. Salt
- ¼ tsp. Pepper

Directions:

1. In mixing bowl, mix together ground chicken, onion, breadcrumbs, garlic, Parmesan cheese, parsley, salt, pepper and egg. Form into golf ball sized meatballs. Refrigerate for approximately 30 minutes.
2. Add chicken broth and ranch dressing seasoning mix to your Instant Pot and stir well to combine. Spray a trivet or steamer rack with non-stick cooking spray. Place trivet into the Instant Pot and place meatballs on the trivet. Lock lid in place

3. Cook on High pressure for approximately 5 minutes. When the timer beeps, do a Natural release for about 5 minutes, then use a Quick pressure release to release any of the remaining pressure. Heat a large-sized skillet on high heat. Add vegetable oil and quickly brown meatballs on two sides.
4. Select Sauté on your Instant Pot and bring chicken broth to a gentle boil. Whisk in cream cheese. In a small-sized bowl, dissolve cornstarch in water and add to the pot. Simmer until sauce thickens. Stir in lemon juice and sour cream
5. Remove your Instant Pot and add meatballs to the sauce and stir well to combine. Allow it to rest 5 minutes before serving. Place over white rice or noodles if you'd like. Garnish with additional parsley if desired. Serve.

French Dip Sandwiches

[Servings: 8]

Ingredients:

- 4 lbs. of Quartered Beef Roast
- 8 Hamburger Buns [White]
- ¾ cups of Soy Sauce
- 1 tbsp. Dried Rosemary
- 1 tsp. Bouillon Beef Granules
- 2 tsp. Black Peppercorns
- 1 tsp. Minced Garlic Clove

Directions:

1. Cut as much of the fat off roast as you can and place it in Instant Pot. Mix together soy sauce, peppercorns, bouillon, garlic and rosemary. Pour mixture over the roast in Instant Pot. Add enough water to cover roast.
2. Lock the cover into place and seal the steam nozzle. Cook on the Beef setting or set manually on High pressure for approximately 35 minutes. Naturally release the pressure. Shred roast with a fork and place on hamburger buns. Serve.

Salmon and Rice with Lemon Caper Chimichurri

[Servings: 4]

Ingredients:

- 1 cup Loosely Packed Parsley
- 1 Lemon [Zested and Juiced]
- 2 Anchovy Fillets [Optional]
- 1 tbsp. Butter
- 2 tbsp. Capers
- 2 tbsp. Olive Oil
- ½ tsp. Crushed Red Pepper
- 1 tsp. Minced Garlic

Rice:

- 1 Finely Minced Shallot
- 1 cup Long-Grain Rice
- ½ cup White Wine
- 1 ¼ cups of Broth
- 1 Lemon [Zested]
- ¼ cup Lemon Juice
- 1 tbsp. Olive Oil
- 1 tbsp. Chopped Parsley
- 1 tsp. Sea Salt

Salmon:

- Lemon Slices
- 4 Salmon Steaks [1-Inch Thick Each]
- Sea Salt
- Ground Pepper

Directions:

1. Make sauce. Combine the olive oil, garlic, anchovy [if using], crushed red pepper and butter in a small-sized saute pan over a medium-high heat

2. Sauté until mixture is fragrant and the garlic is golden. Set to the side. In a small-sized food processor bowl, add parsley, capers, juice and zest of 1 lemon. Spoon olive oil and garlic mixture over the top. Pulse until finely chopped. Scoop into a small-sized bowl until ready to serve.

For Salmon and Rice:

3. In your Instant Pot add olive oil and shallot. Sauté until fragrant. Add rice. Cook for approximately 1 to 2 minutes. Add liquid, zest, parsley, salt and pepper
4. Salt and pepper salmon portions on both sides. Place on steamer basket and top with lemon slices. Set in Instant Pot over the rice and liquid. Lock Instant Pot. Set on Rice setting. Should take about 4 minutes. Remove from the heat source. Release the pressure

To Serve:

5. Lift steamer basket from Instant Pot. Fluff rice with a fork. Plate a scoop of rice. Top with salmon portion. Drizzle with lemon and caper chimichurri. Serve.

Summer Garden Boiled Peanut Salad

[Servings: 2]

Ingredients:

- 1 lb. of Raw Peanuts [Shelled]
- 2 Medium Tomatoes [Chopped]
- ¼ cup Diced Celery
- ¼ cup Finely Diced Hot Peppers
- ½ cup Diced Sweet Onion
- ½ cup Diced Green Pepper
- 2 tbsp. Olive Oil
- 2 tbsp. Fresh Lemon Juice
- 1 Bay Leaf
- ¾ tsp. Salt
- ¼ tsp. Freshly Ground Black Pepper

Directions:

1. To skin peanuts, blanch in boiling salt water for approximately 1 minute, drain. Slip off the skins and discard. To cook peanuts, add to your Instant Pot with 2 cups of water and bay leaf. Cook peanuts for about 20 minutes under pressure or until soft. Drain
2. In a large-sized bowl, combine peanuts with diced vegetables. Whisk together lemon juice, oil, salt and pepper. Pour over salad mixture and toss well to combine. Serve.

Salsa Verde Chicken

[Servings: 4]

Ingredients:

- 2 ½ lbs. of Boneless Chicken Breasts
- 16 ounces of Salsa Verde
- 1 tsp. Cumin
- 1 tsp. Smoked Paprika
- 1 tsp. Kosher Salt

Directions:

1. Place all of the ingredients in Instant Pot. Set the cooker to High pressure for approximately 25 minutes. When timer goes off, quick release the pressure and shred chicken with 2 forks. Serve

Pork Carnitas Burrito Bowls

[Servings: 6]

Ingredients:

- 3 cups of Cooked White Rice
- 14-ounce can of Back Beans

Pork Carnitas:

- 2 ½ lbs. of Trimmed Boneless Pork Shoulder Blade Roast
- 2 Bay Leaves
- 3 Chipotle Peppers in Adobo Sauce
- ¾ cup Reduced Sodium Chicken Broth
- 6 cloves of garlic [Cut into Slivers]
- ¼ tsp. Dry Adobo Seasoning
- ½ tsp. Garlic Powder
- ½ tsp. Sazon
- ¼ tsp. Dry Oregano
- 1 ½ tsp. Cumin
- 2 tsp. Kosher Salt
- Black Pepper

Quick Salsa:

- 10-ounce can of Mild Diced Tomatoes and Green Chilies [Undrained]
- ¼ Chopped Yellow Onion
- 1 clove of Chopped Garlic
- 1 Lime [Juiced]
- ½ cup Cilantro Leaves
- Salt

Toppings: [Optional]

- Shredded Cheddar Cheese
- Chopped Cilantro
- Lime Wedges
- Tortilla Chips
- Sour Cream
- Chopped Green Onions
- Diced Avocado
- Diced Tomatoes

Directions:

1. Season pork with salt and pepper. In a large-sized skillet brown pork on all sides on a high heat for approximately 5 minutes. Remove from the heat and allow to cool.
2. Using sharp knife, insert the blade into pork about 1-inch deep and insert garlic slivers, you'll want to do this all over. Season pork with cumin, oregano, sazon, adobo and garlic powder all over.
3. Pour chicken broth in the crockpot, add chipotle peppers and stir, add bay leaves and place pork in Instant Pot, cover and cook using the pressure cooker setting on High pressure with the Meat button set for 50 minutes.
4. When the pressure releases, shred pork using two forks and combine well with the juices that accumulated at the bottom. Remove bay leaves and adjust cumin and add adobo and mix together well
5. Prepare salsa: Place garlic, tomatoes, cilantro, onion and lime juice in food processor. Pulse until well combined and desired consistency. Add salt.
6. Divide rice evenly among individual serving bowls. Top with black beans and a spoon full of salsa. Add warm pork carnitas and top with some additional salsa. Place toppings on the side and allow everyone to create their own personalized burrito bowl just the way they want it. Serve

Pork Tamales

[**Servings:** 12]

Ingredients:

- 3 lbs. of Boneless Pork Shoulder
- 2 cloves of Smashed Garlic
- 1 Large Onion [Coarsely Chopped]
- 8-ounce package of Dried Corn Husks
- 2 cups of Water
- 2 tbsp. Chili Powder
- 1 tbsp. Chipotle Chili Powder
- 1 tsp. Cumin
- 1 tsp. Salt
- 1 tsp. Pepper

Masa:

- ¼ cup Corn Oil
- ¼ cup Shortening
- 4 cups of Masa
- 1 tsp. Baking Powder
- 2 tsp. Salt

Directions:

1. Place dried corn husks in a large-sized pot [not Instant Pot] and cover with water. Place a heavy plate or a smaller pot full of water on top of the husks to keep them in the water. Allow them to soak for 3 hours or up to 1 day, flipping them occasionally until the husks have softened.
2. Add water, garlic, onion, chili powders, cumin, 1 tsp. salt and pepper and cumin to your Instant Pot and stir well to combine. Add pork and lock lid in place
3. Select High pressure and set timer for approximately 75 minutes. When the beep sounds, turn off your Instant Pot and use a Natural pressure release for about 10 minutes, then use a Quick pressure release to release any of the remaining pressure.
4. When the valve drops carefully remove the lid. Remove meat from the Instant Pot and shred with two forks, discard the excess fat as you're shredding.
5. Strain cooking liquid and reserve to make masa. [I like to place mine in the refrigerator overnight and then discard the fat on top the next day.]
6. Place shredded pork in mixing bowl and season to taste with additional chili powder, salt and cumin. As you season meat, add a small amount of cooking liquid to moisten the meat, but it should not be runny.
7. **Prepare masa filling:** In stand mixer, mix masa, salt, shortening, oil and baking powder. Add remaining reserved cooking liquid with more hot water as needed and beat at a medium or higher until fluffy with a loose cookie dough consistency
8. Place steamer basket in the Instant Pot and add 2 cups of water. Unfold 2 corn husks onto work surface. Take ¼ cup masa and starting near the top of the husk, press it out into a 4-inch square leaving 2 to 3 inches at the bottom of husk
9. Place a tbsp. filling in a line down the center of masa. Fold the sides until they just begin to overlap and wrap the husk around dough. Fold up the bottom part of husk.
10. Stand them up in the steamer. Cook on High pressure for approximately 20 minutes. Do a Natural pressure release for about 10 minutes, then use a Quick release to release any of the remaining pressure. Serve

Spanish Brown Rice

[**Servings:** 8]

Ingredients:
- 1 Medium Yellow Onion [Diced]
- 3 cups of Organic Chicken Stock
- 2 cups of Long Grain Brown Rice
- 4 cloves of Minced Garlic
- 2 tbsp. Coconut Oil
- 2 tbsp. Tomato Paste
- 1 tbsp. Dried Oregano
- 1 tsp. Sea Salt

Directions:
1. Heat the inner liner of your Instant Pot on the "Sauté" setting. Melt coconut oil. Add onion; sauté approximately 5 minutes until translucent. Add garlic, oregano and tomato paste; stir and allow to sauté for approximately 1 to 2 minutes.
2. Add brown rice; stir well to combine and allow to cook for another minute or so. It will begin to caramelize a little bit.
3. Add chicken stock and sea salt. Give it a good stir. Place the lid on your Instant Pot and lock it into place. Press the Manual button and cook for approximately 15 minutes. When done and pressure has naturally released, remove lid. Serve.

Moroccan Sticky Chicken

[**Servings:** 2]

Ingredients:
- 1 lb. of Chicken Drumsticks
- 1 Medium Lemon [Zested and Juiced]
- ½ cup Bone Broth
- ¼ cup Honey
- ½ tsp. Ground Cinnamon
- ¼ tsp. Packed Saffron Threads
- ¼ tsp. Ground Coriander
- 2 tsp. Blackstrap Molasses
- 1 tsp. Garlic Powder
- ½ tsp. Ground Ginger
- 1 tsp. Ground Cumin
- 1 tsp. Paprika
- 1 tsp. Sea Salt
- ½ tsp. Black pepper
- Sesame Seeds [For Garnish]
- Chopped Scallions [For Garnish]

Directions:
1. Pat the chicken dry with paper towels. Make spice rub by combining paprika, garlic powder, ginger, cumin, coriander, cinnamon, saffron, sea salt and black pepper. Coat chicken with the rub well on all sides. Set your Instant Pot to Sauté with lid off. When it reads "Hot," grease the bottom with a small amount of oil. Brown drumsticks on all sides, about 15 minutes in total
2. Add broth to pot. Turn the Instant Pot to "Keep Warm/Cancel" and put lid on. Set to Manual and move the time to approximately 10 minutes. Make sure the steam valve is set to "Sealing," as we are using pressure to cook drumsticks
3. After drumsticks have finished, press the "Keep Warm/Cancel" to turn it off. Release the pressure by moving the steam valve to "Venting." Always use caution as the steam is hot. Note: do not use the optional natural steam release here, as it can cause the chicken to continue to overcook and become dry
4. Remove lid and with tongs, carefully move chicken to a large-sized bowl and cover it tightly with foil to keep warm. Leave juices rendered from the cooking process in the pan. Turn your Instant Pot to "Sauté" again and keep the lid off.
5. In a small-sized bowl, whisk together honey, molasses, lemon juice and zest. Pour into pot with the reserved cooking juices. When the indicator hits "Hot," you should have a rolling boil. Whisk occasionally [being cautious of the steam] until liquid has reduced to a thick sauce. Should take approximately 5 to 10 minutes.
6. Coat drumsticks with the sauce. Garnish with sesame seeds and chopped scallions, as desired. Serve.

Pork Vindaloo

[**Servings:** 6]

Ingredients:

- 3 lbs. of Boneless Pork Butt Roast [Trimmed and Cut into 1-Inch Pieces]
- 14.5-ounce can of Diced Tomatoes
- ¼ cup Minced Fresh Cilantro
- ¼ cup All-Purpose Flour
- 1 cup Low-Sodium Chicken Broth
- 8 cloves of Minced Garlic
- 3 Finely Chopped Onions
- 1 tbsp. Paprika
- 2 tbsp. Red Wine Vinegar
- 2 tbsp. Vegetable Oil
- 1 tbsp. Mustard Seeds
- ¼ tsp. Cayenne Pepper
- 1 tsp. Ground Cumin
- 1/8 tsp. Ground Cloves
- 1 tsp. Sugar
- Salt
- Pepper

Directions:

1. Pat pork dry with paper towels and season with salt and pepper. Heat 1 tbsp. oil in your Instant Pot over a medium-high heat until just smoking. Brown half of meat on all sides, about 8 minutes. Transfer to bowl.
2. Heat remaining 1 tbsp. oil in the now-empty pot over a medium heat until shimmering. Add onions and ¼ tsp. salt and cook until softened. Should take about 5 minutes
3. Stir in garlic, mustard seeds, paprika, cayenne, cumin and cloves and cook just until fragrant, about 30 seconds. Stir in flour and cook for approximately 1 minute. Whisk in broth, scraping up any browned bits and smoothing out any lumps
4. Stir in tomatoes, sugar, vinegar, browned pork with any accumulated juices and remaining pork. Cook on High pressure for approximately 30 minutes. Lock your Instant Pot lid in place and bring to high heat pressure. As soon as pot reaches high pressure, reduce heat to medium-low and cook for approximately 30 minutes, adjusting heat as needed to maintain high pressure
5. Naturally release pressure. Remove pot from heat and allow the pressure to release naturally for 15 minutes. Quick release any remaining pressure, then carefully remove the lid, allowing steam to escape away from you. Using a large spoon, skim the excess fat from the surface of the soup. Stir in cilantro, season with salt and pepper to taste. Serve.

Bahn Mi Sliders

[**Servings:** 12]

Ingredients:

- ½ lb. of Peeled Baby Carrots
- ½ lb. of Radishes
- 1 cup Cider Vinegar
- ½ cup Water
- 1 Large Chunk of Peeled Ginger
- 3 tbsp. Sugar
- 1 tbsp. Salt

Pork:

- 2 lbs. of Pork Tenderloin
- 1 cup Water
- 1 Finely Chopped Scallion
- 1 piece of Minced Ginger
- 2 cloves of Minced Garlic
- 2 tbsp. Maple Syrup
- 3 tbsp. Fish Sauce
- 2 tbsp. Soy Sauce
- 1 tbsp. Brown Sugar
- 1 tsp. Sesame Oil
- ½ tsp. Freshly Ground Black Pepper

Other Ingredients:

- 1 cup Mayonnaise
- 12 Hawaiian Dinner Rolls
- 12 Lettuce Leaves
- Sriracha Hot Sauce

Directions:

1. Cut carrots and radishes into matchstick sized pieces. Cut ginger into very thin slices. In a medium-sized saucepan combine water, vinegar, sugar and salt. Bring to a boil and remove from the heat. Add carrots, radishes and ginger to the hot vinegar. Cover and allow it to cool for approximately 30 minutes before transferring to refrigerator to chill. Drain immediately
2. Cut pork into 2 large-sized chunks and pat dry. Place pork in your Instant Pot with remaining pork ingredients. Lock lid into place and cook on High pressure for approximately 50 minutes.
3. Allow the steam to release naturally. When the pressure valve drops, remove lid, tilting it away from face to allow residual steam to escape. Test the meat by prodding it with a fork, it should be easy to pull apart.
4. Transfer cooked meat to a cutting board and allow it to stand until cool enough to handle, then shred using two forks to pull apart. Pour any liquid from the pot over meat
5. Cut open a roll and spread both sides with a small amount of mayonnaise. Top with a portion of pulled pork and pickled vegetables and then add a lettuce leaf. Season the top bun with Sriracha if so desired. Repeat this process for the remaining sliders. Serve

Sirloin Tips in Gravy

[Servings: 6-8]

Ingredients:

- 5 lbs. of Sirloin Tip Roast [Cubed]
- 1 Diced Onion
- ½ cup Flour
- 2 cups of Beef Broth
- 1 ½ cups of Water
- 4 tbsp. Vegetable Oil

Directions:

1. Add 1 tbsp. oil to your Instant Pot and select the Sauté setting. When oil is hot, brown meat in small batches, do not crowd. When all meat is browned, add onion to your Instant Pot and saute until tender about 3 minutes
2. Add browned meat and beef broth to onion in Instant Pot, cover and lock the lid in place. Select High pressure and set for approximately 15 minutes cook time. When the cook time ends, use a Quick pressure release.
3. Mix flour and water to make a slurry to thicken broth. Add slurry to cooked meat and broth in Instant Pot. Select Sauté and bring to a boil. Boil for a few minutes until broth is thickened. Add salt and pepper to taste. Serve.

Sloppy Lasagna

[Servings: 6]

Ingredients:

Meat Ragu Sauce:

- 1 lb. of Ground Beef Chuck
- 1 Medium Yellow Onion [Finely Chopped]
- 1 Fresh Thyme Sprig
- 1 Medium Carrot [Finely Chopped]
- 1 Fresh Oregano Sprig
- 1 cup Chopped Tomatoes
- 2 cloves of Crushed Garlic
- 1 Celery Stick [Finely Chopped]
- ½ cup Tomato Puree
- ½ cup Water
- 1 tbsp. Olive Oil
- 2 tbsp. Unsalted Butter
- ½ tsp. Salt
- ¼ tsp. Freshly Ground Black Pepper

Lasagna:

- 8 ounces of Wavy Lasagna Noodles [Broken into 2-Inch Pieces]
- 8 ounces of Diced Mozzarella Cheese
- 1 tsp. Salt
- Water [As Needed]

Directions:

For Sauce:

1. Select Sauté and add 1 tbsp. butter and olive oil to Instant Pot. When butter has melted, add onion, oregano, thyme, salt and pepper, stirring occasionally, until onion has softened. Stir in carrot and celery.
2. Move the contents to the side of Instant Pot. Add beef and garlic and stir to break up. Sauté, stirring occasionally, until the beef is brown on at least one side and the juices have evaporated. Should take about 5 minutes. Pour in crushed tomatoes.
3. Close and lock the lid of Instant Pot. Cook at High pressure for approximately 18 minutes. When the beep sounds turn the Instant Pot off and use a Quick pressure release. When the valve drops carefully remove lid. Remove and discard herb stems. Add remaining 1 tbsp. butter to sauce and stir until melted.

For Lasagna:

4. Add salt and lasagna strips to sauce in the Instant Pot. Pour in enough water to cover pasta. Smooth down the top pieces of pasta so they are submerged.
5. Close and lock the lid of Instant Pot. Cook at Low pressure for approximately 5 minutes or half the cooking time indicated on the pasta package.
6. When the beep sounds turn the Instant Pot off and use a Quick pressure release. When the valve drops carefully remove lid. Taste the noodles and if you'd like them a little softer, cook on simmer until noodles are tender
7. Pour lasagna into a large-sized serving dish. Sprinkle mozzarella over the lasagna. Stir and allow to stand, uncovered, for 2 minutes before serving. Serve.

Salsa Lime Chicken with Mozzarella

[Servings: 4]

Ingredients:

- 4 Large Boneless Skinless Chicken Breasts [Frozen]
- 1 cup Grated Low-Fat Mozzarella
- 1 cup Tomato Sauce
- 1 cup Mild or Medium Salsa
- 2 Limes [Juiced]
- ½ tsp. Salt
- ¼ tsp. Pepper

Directions:

1. Add salsa, tomato sauce, chicken, salt, pepper and lime juice to Instant Pot. Cover and lock lid in place. Select High pressure and set the timer for 12 minutes cook time. When the timer beeps, turn off and use a Quick pressure release. Check and make sure chicken is cooked to 165 degrees.
2. Preheat broiler and spray a small-sized glass casserole dish with non-stick cooking spray. Place chicken in the dish. Select Sauté and cook sauce, stirring frequently until sauce is desired consistency. Spoon sauce over chicken
3. Sprinkle 1 cup grated low-fat Mozzarella on top of chicken and sauce, put dish in the oven and broil until cheese is melted and starting to brown. Should take about 5 minutes, but watch it carefully. Serve.

Korean Beef

[Servings: 6]

Ingredients:

- 4 lbs. of Bottom Roast [Cut into Cubes]
- 1 Granny Smith Apple [Peeled and Chopped]
- Large Orange [Juiced]
- 1 cup Beef Broth
- ½ cup Soy Sauce
- 2 tbsp. Olive Oil
- 5 cloves of Minced Garlic
- 1 tbsp. Fresh Grated Ginger
- Salt
- Pepper

Directions:

1. Season cubed roast liberally with salt and pepper. Heat your Instant Pot to Sauté. Once pan is hot, coat pan with the olive oil and in batches brown meat on all the sides. Transfer meat to a plate while you're working
2. Once all meat is browned de-glaze the pan with beef broth, scraping up all the browned bits. Pour in soy sauce and stir well to combine.
3. Return all meat back to the pan and then place garlic, ginger and apple on top of meat, stirring lightly to slightly combine. Add in orange juice
4. Place the lid on your Instant Pot and using the Manual button on High pressure set to approximately 45 minutes. Make sure that the valve is closed. Once you're done cooking, release the steam and shred meat using a fork. Serve.

Cauliflower Fettuccine Alfredo

[Servings: 4-6]

Ingredients:

- 1 lb. of Fettuccine Pasta [Whole-Grain]
- 2 cups of Spinach [Coarsely Chopped]
- 8 cups of Cauliflower Florets
- 1 cup Chicken or Vegetable Broth
- 2 Finely Chopped Green Onions
- 2 cloves of Garlic
- 2 tbsp. Butter
- 2 tsp. Salt

Garnish:

- Gorgonzola Cheese
- Sun-Dried Tomatoes [Chopped]
- Balsamic Glaze

Directions:

1. Select Sauté on your Instant Pot and add butter. When melted, add garlic cloves and saute until fragrant, should take about 2 minutes, stirring constantly so garlic doesn't burn
2. Add cauliflower, broth and salt. Secure lid and turn the pressure release knob to a closed/sealing position. Cook at High pressure for approximately 6 minutes
3. While cauliflower is cooking, heat a pot of water to boiling on stove top. Add pasta and cook until al dente. Reserve about 1 cup water and then drain pasta. Return pasta to the empty pot. When cooking is complete, use a 10-minute Natural release
4. Blend with an immersion blender right in pot until very smooth and silky, or carefully transfer to a blender and puree until smooth. By hand, stir in chopped spinach and green onions and allow hot sauce to wilt the spinach.
5. Pour sauce over the pasta and toss. Add a half cup or so of reserved pasta water to the pasta if needed. The starchy water will help the sauce to stick to pasta. Garnish with Gorgonzola cheese, sun-dried tomatoes and a drizzle of balsamic vinegar. Serve.

Coq Au Vin

[Servings: 6]

Ingredients:

- 3 lbs. of Boneless Skinless Chicken Thighs [Well Trimmed]
- 12-ounce package of White Mushrooms [Quartered]
- 2 cloves of Chopped Garlic
- 1 Medium Chopped Yellow Onion
- 1 Bay Leaf
- 2 Sliced Carrots
- ½ cup Diced Bacon
- 1 cup Chicken Broth
- 1 cup Red Wine
- 2 sprigs of Thyme
- 2 tbsp. Cornstarch
- 3 tbsp. Cold Water
- 2 tbsp. Chopped Parsley
- 1 tbsp. Tomato Paste
- 1 tbsp. Butter
- 1 tbsp. Vegetable Oil
- Salt
- Pepper

Directions:

1. Select Browning and add diced bacon to Instant Pot. Brown bacon until crisp, stirring frequently. Remove bacon to a plate, leaving bacon fat in the pot. Season chicken with pepper and salt. Add chicken to the pot and brown on both sides in bacon fat. Remove chicken to a platter, leaving fat in the pan
2. Add onions and cook, stirring frequently, until softened and lightly caramelized. Add garlic and cook for approximately 1 minute.
3. Add wine to deglaze the pot and let it almost completely evaporate to concentrate the flavor and remove most of liquid

4. Stir in chicken broth, bay leaf, tomato paste, thyme and carrots. Add browned chicken to pot, along with any juices that have collected on platter. Cover the pot and lock lid in place.
5. Select High pressure and set the timer for 10 minutes cook time. [It will take about 10 minutes to reach high pressure]
6. While chicken is cooking, heat a large-sized saute pan over a medium-high heat until hot. Add oil and butter. When butter is melted, add mushrooms and cook until golden. Season with salt and pepper.
7. When the timer beeps, do a Quick pressure release and remove chicken from the Instant Pot to a serving dish.
8. Combine cornstarch and water, whisking until smooth. Add cornstarch mixture into the sauce in Instant Pot, stirring constantly
9. Select Simmer and bring to a boil, stirring constantly. After sauce thickens, add mushrooms and stir to coat with sauce. Adjust seasoning if desired. Combine sauce with chicken in the serving bowl. Serve topped with crumbled bacon and chopped parsley. Serve.

Shredded Beef Enchiladas

[Servings: 10]

Ingredients:

- 3 lbs. of Chuck Beef Roast
- 10 (6-inch) Flour or Corn Tortillas
- 1 ½ cups of Shredded Mexican Cheese Blend
- 1 cup Salsa
- 1 ½ cups of Beef Broth
- 3 tbsp. Water
- 2 tbsp. Apple Cider Vinegar
- 1 tsp. Onion Powder
- 1 tsp. Ground Cumin
- 1 tsp. Chili Powder
- 1 tsp. Garlic Powder
- 2 tbsp. Cornstarch
- 1 tsp. Salt
- ½ tsp. Pepper

Directions:

1. Mix together broth, salsa, vinegar, chili powder, cumin, onion powder, garlic powder, salt and pepper in Instant Pot. Add beef. Select High pressure and set timer for approximately 75 minutes
2. When the beep sounds, turn off your Instant Pot and use a Natural pressure release for 10 minutes and then do a Quick pressure release to release the remaining pressure. When the valve drops carefully remove the lid.
3. Remove beef from your Instant Pot and shred with two forks, discard any fat as you shredded. Use turkey baster or fat separator to remove excess fat from cooking liquid
4. In a small-sized bowl, whisk together cornstarch and 3 tbsp. water. Add to liquid in Instant Pot. Select Sauté and cook, stirring constantly, until sauce is thickened slightly
5. Mix ½ cup sauce with the shredded beef. Spread ½ cup sauce on the bottom of a 9 x 13-inch pan sprayed with non-stick cooking spray.
6. Fill each tortilla with ⅓ cup shredded beef mixture and 1 tbsp. cheese. Roll up and place the seam side down in pan. Pour sauce over the enchiladas
7. Top with any remaining cheese and bake at 350 degrees for 20 to 30 minutes until bubbly and hot. Let the enchiladas rest for approximately 5 to 10 minutes before serving. Add sour cream, guacamole and fresh salsa, if so desired. Serve.

Merlot Beef and Vegetables

[**Servings:** 10]

Ingredients:

- 3 lbs. of Stew Beef
- ½ cup Kettle and Fire's Beef Bone Broth
- 1 cup Green Beans [Halved]
- ⅔ cup Merlot Red Wine
- 8 cups of Sliced Fingerling Potato
- 3 cups of Yellow Onion Chunks
- 1 ¼ cups of Sliced Carrot
- 2 tbsp. Apple Cider Vinegar
- 1 tsp. Cinnamon
- 1 tsp. Sea Salt
- 1 tsp. Black Pepper

Directions:

1. Place all of ingredients in Instant Pot. Lock cover into place and seal the steam nozzle. Press the Meat / Stew setting or set manually on High pressure for approximately 35 minutes
2. Naturally release the pressure for about 5 minutes, then Quick release any of the remaining pressure. Serve.

Dinner Recipes

Mongolian Beef

[Servings: 4]

Ingredients:

- 1 ½ lbs. of Sliced Flank Steak
- ¼ cup Arrowroot
- ¾ cup Coconut Aminos
- ½ cup Grated Carrot
- ¾ cup Honey
- ¾ cup Water
- ⅓ cup Green Onion [Scallion]
- 2 tbsp. Olive Oil
- ½ tsp. Peeled and Minced Fresh Ginger

Directions:

1. Coat flank steak with arrowroot powder. Combine olive oil, honey, ginger, water, coconut aminos, carrots and green onions and add to Instant Pot. Place flank steak in Instant Pot. Lock the cover into place and seal the steam nozzle
2. Set on the Meat/ Stew setting or set manually for approximately 35 minutes. Naturally release pressure for about 5 minutes and Quick release any of the remaining pressure. Serve.

Sausage and Pasta

[Servings: 4]

Ingredients:

- 1 lb. of Penne Pasta
- 1 lb. of Sausage Meat
- 2 cups of Tomato Puree
- 2 cloves of Minced Garlic
- ¼ cup Freshly Grated Parmesan
- 1 Chopped Onion
- 3 ½ ounces of Lardon
- 1 tbsp. Olive Oil
- Freshly Chopped Basil [Handful]
- Salt
- Water

Directions:

1. Set your Instant Pot on Sauté. Once it says Hot, add olive oil. Render lardon for about 3 to 4 minutes. Remove the lardon onto plate. Brown sausage meat until cooked through
2. Add onion and garlic and sauté them for a few minutes, scraping up the brown bits from the bottom of pot. Cancel the Sauté mode. Pour in the tomato puree and salt
3. Add dry pasta and stir to coat, then flatten until level. Add enough water to just cover the pasta.
4. Close and lock lid, making sure the sealing knob is on sealing. Choose the manual, low-pressure setting for 5 minutes
5. Once the cooking is done, release the pressure by using the Quick pressure release. Stir in chopped basil and Parmesan cheese. Serve.

Cranberry Beef Roast

[**Servings:** 4]

Ingredients:

- 2 ½ lbs. of Quartered Beef Roast
- 12 ounces of Fresh Cranberries
- ½ cup Orange Juice
- ½ cup Sugar
- ½ cup Brown Sugar
- ½ cup Water
- 1 tbsp. Dried Minced Onion
- ¼ tsp. Cinnamon

Directions:

1. Combine cranberries, water, orange juice, brown sugar, cinnamon and white sugar together in Instant Pot. Mix together well
2. Sauté for 5 minutes until cranberries start to burst. Add roast and dried onions. Lock the lid into place and seal the steam nozzle. Cook on Manual for approximately 40 minutes. Release pressure naturally for about 15 minutes. Remove roast and cranberries with slotted spoon. Serve

Sweet and Sour Meatballs

[**Servings:** 6]

Ingredients:

- 1 lb. of Ground Beef
- 2 cups of Canned Chunks Pineapple
- ½ cup Brown Sugar
- 1 cup Diced Red Bell Pepper
- 1 cup Bread Crumbs
- 1 cup Diced Onion
- ½ cup Ketchup
- ½ cup Rice Vinegar
- 1 Egg
- 1 cup Diced Green Bell Pepper
- ¼ cup Water
- 2 tbsp. Soy Sauce
- 2 tbsp. Cornstarch
- 1/8 tsp. Salt
- 1/8 tsp. Black Pepper

Directions:

1. Mix together ground beef, onion, egg and breadcrumbs. Form mixture into meatballs about 1.5-inches in size. Mix together rice vinegar, ketchup, pineapple with juice, brown sugar and soy sauce
2. Place meatballs and sauce in Instant Pot. Lock lid in place and seal the steam nozzle. Cook on Manual for approximately 6 minutes.
3. Natural release the pressure for about 5 minutes. Remove the lid. Turn off. Dissolve corn starch in water. Add this and peppers to the contents in Instant Pot
4. Sauté for approximately 5 minutes or until thickened. Turn off saute by keeping warm or turning off completely. Serve.

Apple Pie Pork Chops

[Servings: 4]

Ingredients:

- 1 ½ lbs. of Boneless Pork Chops
- 6 cups of Peeled and Sliced Apple
- ¾ cup Sugar
- ½ cup Water
- 2 tbsp. All-Purpose Flour
- ½ tsp. Ground Cloves
- 1 tsp. Cinnamon
- ½ tsp. Ground Allspice

Directions:

1. Mix together apples, flour, sugar, cinnamon, cloves and allspice. Place pork chops in the bottom of Instant Pot. Add apple mixture on top of pork. Lock the lid in place and seal the steam nozzle.
2. Set on Manual for approximately 10 minutes. Natural release for 5 minutes then Quick release any of the remaining pressure. Remove pork chops and spoon apples over the top. Serve.

Barbeque Ribs

[Servings: 2]

Ingredients:

- 1 rack of Baby Back Ribs
- Ground Black Pepper
- 4 tbsp. BBQ Sauce
- Kosher Salt

Directions:

1. Remove the membrane from the back of ribs with a paper towel. Season ribs with a generous amount of kosher salt and ground black pepper.
2. Place 1 cup cold running tap water and the trivet into Instant Pot. Place baby back ribs on top of trivet. Close the lid and cook at High pressure for approximately 16 to 25 minutes.
3. Adjust timing according to preference: 16 minutes [tender with a bit of chew] to 25 minutes [fall off the bone]. Turn off heat and perform a full Natural release. Open lid carefully
4. While baby back ribs are cooking in your Instant Pot preheat oven to 450 degrees. Brush favorite BBQ sauce all over baby back ribs on all sides including the bones. Place baby back ribs with the baking tray in oven for 10 to 15 minutes. Remove ribs from the oven. Serve.

Italian Beef

[Servings: 6]

Ingredients:

- 3 ½ lbs. of Quartered Beef Roast
- 16 ounces of Canned Whole Tomatoes
- 2 whole Bay Leaf
- ¼ cup Water
- 1 tbsp. Wine Vinegar
- 2 tsp. Bouillon Beef Granules
- ½ tsp. Pickling Spice
- 3 ½ tsp. Minced Garlic Cloves
- 1 tsp. Salt
- ¼ tsp. Black Pepper

Directions:

1. Trim the fat from meat and cut beef to fit inside Instant Pot. Place all of other ingredients into your Instant Pot over the beef. Lock the cover into place and seal the steam nozzle.
2. Select the Meat / Stew setting or manually set for approximately 35 minutes
3. Naturally release pressure for 5 minutes then Quick release any of the remaining pressure. Remove the bay leaf. Serve.

Pulled Pork Loaded Sweet Potatoes

[Servings: 6]

Ingredients:

- 2 lbs. of Quartered Pork Roast
- 1 cup Diced Onion
- 1 cup Peeled and Diced Apple
- 1 cup Chopped Kale
- 1 cup Water
- ½ cup Cooked and Diced Bacon
- 6 Medium Cooked Sweet Potato
- 2 ⅔ fluid ounces of Apple Cider Vinegar
- 2 tbsp. Bacon Fat
- 2 tbsp. Melted Coconut Oil
- 1 tbsp. Peeled and Minced Fresh Ginger
- ½ tsp. Cinnamon
- 1 tsp. Turmeric
- ½ tsp. Fresh Cilantro
- ½ tsp. Sea Salt

Directions:

1. Place pork roast in Instant Pot. Mix together coconut oil, apple, onion, apple cider vinegar, ginger, water, cinnamon, turmeric and sea salt. Pour mixture over the pork. Lock the lid in place and seal the steam nozzle
2. Cook on the Manual setting for approximately 50 minutes. Natural release for 5 minutes then Quick release any of the remaining pressure
3. Shred the pork and add cilantro. Cut part way into each sweet potato lengthwise to open and gently smash down with fork. Divide potatoes cut sides up among baking dishes.
4. Divide pork mixture between potatoes [about ⅓ cup per potato]. Be sure to spoon any extra juices onto potatoes as well
5. Heat bacon grease in skillet over a medium heat. Toss kale into the bacon grease and fry until dark green and crispy.
6. Drain kale on a paper towel. Top potatoes with bacon and kale. Bake, uncovered, at 350 degrees for approximately 20 minutes until heated through. Serve.

Meatballs

[Servings: 8]

Ingredients:

- 2 lbs. of Ground Beef
- ¼ cup Chopped Fresh Parsley
- ½ cup Bread Crumbs
- ½ cup Diced Onion
- 4 cups of Marinara Sauce
- ¼ cup Shredded Parmesan Cheese
- 4 Eggs [Beaten]
- 2 tsp. Minced Garlic Cloves
- 1 tsp. Red Pepper Flakes
- 1 tsp. Salt
- ½ tsp. Black Pepper

Directions:

1. In a large-sized mixing bowl combine raw ground beef, garlic, eggs, onion, breadcrumbs, red pepper, parsley, salt, pepper and Parmesan. Use hands to get it thoroughly combined
2. Roll meat mixture into balls about 2-inches in diameter. Place meatballs in your Instant Pot and cover with sauce. Lock lid into place and seal the steam nozzle. Cook on Manual setting for approximately 6 minutes. Natural release pressure for 5 minutes. Serve.

Braised Short Ribs

[**Servings:** 8]

Ingredients:

- 4 lbs. of Beef Short Ribs
- 2 individual Fresh Thyme
- ⅔ cup Ketchup
- 2 ½ cups of Diced Onion
- 1 cup Red Wine
- 1 tbsp. Olive Oil
- 2 tbsp. Worcestershire Sauce
- 3 tbsp. Soy Sauce
- 2 tbsp. Brown Sugar
- 2 tsp. Minced Garlic Cloves
- 1 tsp. Salt
- ½ tsp. Black Pepper

Directions:

1. Sprinkle ribs with salt and pepper. Set your Instant Pot to Sauté and heat the olive oil. Sear ribs on all sides in your Instant Pot and remove. Add onions and cook until translucent.
2. Add garlic and cook for approximately 1 more minute. Place ribs back into the pot.
3. In bowl, whisk wine, soy sauce, ketchup, Worcestershire sauce and brown sugar. Pour over ribs. Place sprigs of thyme on top of ribs. Lock the cover into place and seal the steam nozzle
4. Set to the Meat / Stew setting or set manually for approximately 35 minutes. Naturally release pressure for 5 minutes then Quick release any of the remaining pressure. Remove thyme sprigs. Serve.

Osso Bucco

[**Servings:** 4]

Ingredients:

- 2 lbs. of Red Potatoes [Washed]
- 4 Veal or Lamb Shanks [Cut to Size]
- 2 stalks of Celery [Cut into Large Chunks]
- 2 Medium Carrots [Chopped in Large Chunks]
- 2 cups of Chicken Broth
- 2 cloves of Crushed Garlic
- ¼ cup Flour
- 1 Medium Onion [Chopped]
- ¼ cup Olive Oil
- 1 tbsp. Butter
- 2 tbsp. Butter
- 1 tsp. Thyme
- ½ tsp. Onion Powder
- ½ tsp. Garlic Powder
- 1 tsp. Rosemary
- ½ tsp. Black Pepper
- ½ tsp. Salt

Directions:

1. Add flour and the seasonings to a large-sized bowl. Use a wire whisk to blend everything together. Rinse shanks and dry with paper towel. Roll each shank in flour mix and set to the side on plate [Keep the remaining flour]
2. Preheat a large-sized skillet. Add oil and bring to almost smoking. Place shanks in the skillet and brown turning each shank to brown on all sides of shank. Once they are browned, set to the side. Add flour to the remaining oil and make a rue. Once rue is made add broth to loosen the rue into a sauce
3. Pour ½ of sauce into your Instant Pot and place each shank into sauce standing upright. Fill in the gaps with vegetables. Pour remaining sauce over shanks and vegetables. Seal the Instant Pot and cook for approximately 90 minutes
4. Towards the end of cooking cycle, boil red potatoes [skin on] until tender. Mash potatoes adding butter. Add salt and pepper to taste. Place lamb shank on bed of potatoes. Add a large spoon of vegetables. Ladle on some of sauce from the cooker over shank, vegetables and potatoes. Serve.

Corned Beef and Cabbage

[**Servings:** 6]

Ingredients:

- 4 lbs. of Corned Beef Brisket
- 1 ½ lbs. of Medium Red Potatoes
- 3 Black Peppercorns
- 3 cloves of Garlic [Peeled and Smashed]
- 1 head of Cabbage [Cut into Wedges]
- 1 Small Onion [Peeled and Quartered]
- 5 Medium Carrots [Peeled and Cut into Chunks]
- 4 cups of Water
- 2 Bay Leaves
- ½ tsp. Whole Allspice Berries
- 1 tsp. Dried Thyme

Directions:

1. Place corned beef, garlic cloves, water, onion quarters, peppercorns, allspice and thyme in Instant Pot. Lock lid in place and press the Manual and set time for approximately 90 minutes
2. When cooking is complete, switch your Instant Pot off and allow the pressure to release naturally for 10 minutes, then Quick release any of the remaining pressure.
3. Remove the meat from the liquid and transfer to plate. Cover with tin foil and allow to rest for 15 minutes while you prepare vegetables
4. Add potatoes, carrots and cabbage to liquid in your Instant Pot and lock the lid in place. Press Manual and set time for approximately 10 minutes.
5. When cooking is complete, Quick release the pressure. Use a slotted spoon to remove vegetables. Add over corned beef and add liquid to moisten the meat as needed. Serve

Turkey with Gravy

[**Servings:** 6]

Ingredients:

- 5 lb. of Bone-In Skin-On Turkey Breast
- 1 ½ cups of Bone Broth
- ¼ cup Dry White Wine
- 1 Large Carrot [Cut into Medium Dice]
- 1 Medium Onion [Cut into Medium Dice]
- 1 clove of Garlic [Peeled and Smashed]
- 1 Celery Rib [Cut into Medium Dice]
- 2 tsp. Dried Sage
- 2 tbsp. Ghee or Butter
- 1 Bay Leaf
- Salt
- Black Pepper

Directions:

1. Pat turkey breast dry and generously season with salt and pepper. Melt cooking fat in Instant Pot. Use the Sauté function. Brown turkey breast, skin side down. Should take about 5 minutes and transfer to a plate, leaving fat in pot
2. Add onion, carrot and celery to pot and cook in your Instant Pot on the Sauté function until softened. Should take about 5 minutes. Stir in garlic and sage and cook until fragrant. Should take about 30 seconds
3. Pour in wine and cook until slightly reduced. Should take about 3 minutes. Stir in broth and bay leaf. Using a wooden spoon, scrape up all of browned bits stuck on the bottom of pot
4. Place turkey skin side up in pot with any accumulated juices. Lock the lid in place and set your Instant Pot for 35 minutes on High pressure.
5. Use the Quick release method and carefully remove lid. Transfer turkey breast to carving board or plate and tent loosely with foil, allowing it to rest while you prepare gravy.
6. Use an immersion blender or carefully transfer cooking liquid and vegetables to blender and puree until smooth. Return to a medium-high heat and cook until thickened and reduced to about 2 cups. Adjust seasoning to taste. Slice turkey breast and add hot gravy on top. Serve

Rack of Lamb Casserole

[Servings: 8]

Ingredients:

- 1 lb. Rack of Lamb
- 1 lb. of Baby Potatoes
- 2 stalks of Celery
- 2 cups of Chicken Stock
- 4 cloves of Garlic
- 1 Large Onion
- 2 Carrots
- 2 Medium Tomatoes
- 2 tbsp. Ketchup
- 3 tbsp. Sherry or Red Wine
- 2 tsp. Cumin Powder
- 2 tsp. Salt
- 2 tsp. Paprika
- Pinch of Dried Oregano Leaves
- Pinch of Dried Rosemary
- Splash of Beer [Optional]

Directions:

1. Wash all of vegetables and cut potatoes and carrots into 1-inch cubes. Dice tomatoes, onion and garlic. Cut the rack of lamb into two halves. Put everything in cooking pot and mix together well. Put pot into Instant Pot. Close the lid and press the Stew / Meat button. Cook for 35 minutes
2. Once finished cooking, wait a few minutes until your Instant Pot cools down and you can safely or comfortably release the remaining pressure by turning the pressure release handle to the "Vent" position. You can open the lid safely once there is no pressure inside. Serve

Marinated Steak

[Servings: 4]

Ingredients:

- 2 lbs. of Flank Steak
- ¼ cup Apple Cider Vinegar
- ½ cup Olive Oil
- 1 tbsp. Worcestershire Sauce
- 2 tbsp. Dried Onion Soup Mix

Directions:

1. Set your Instant Pot to Sauté. Add flank steak and brown on each side. Add vinegar, Worcestershire, olive oil and onion soup mix. Lock the cover into place and seal the steam nozzle
2. Set on the Meat / Stew setting or set manually for approximately 35 minutes. Naturally release pressure for about 5 minutes and Quick release any of the remaining pressure. Serve.

Lamb Shanks with Figs and Ginger

[Servings: 4]

Ingredients:

- 4 (12-ounce) Lamb Shanks
- 3 cloves of Finely Minced Garlic
- 1 ½ cups of Bone Broth
- 1 Sliced Thinly Large Onion
- 2 tbsp. Coconut Oil
- 2 tbsp. Minced Fresh Ginger
- 2 tbsp. Coconut Aminos
- 2 tbsp. Apple Cider Vinegar
- 2 tsp. Fish Sauce
- 10 Dried Figs [Stems Cut Off and Halved Lengthwise]

Directions:

1. Turn your Instant Pot on and press the Sauté button. When hot, add 1 tbsp. coconut oil. Place two of lamb shanks in the pot and brown on all sides, turning occasionally. Transfer to plate or bowl. Repeat with remaining tbsp. coconut oil and lamb shanks.

2. Add onion and ginger to empty pot and cook, stirring often, until softened. Should take about 3 minutes. Stir in coconut aminos, vinegar, fish sauce and garlic. Stir in broth and figs, scraping up any of the browned bits.
3. Return the shanks and any accumulated juices to Instant Pot. Make sure the meaty portion of each shank is at least partially submerged in the liquid. Lock the lid in place. Set your Instant Pot to cook at High pressure for approximately 1 hour.
4. Turn off Instant Pot, do not allow it to go into keep-warm setting and let the pressure return to normal naturally for approximately 20 to 30 minutes
5. Unlock and open Instant Pot. Transfer shanks to serving platter. Skim the surface fat from sauce in your Instant Pot and discard. Ladle sauce over the shanks. Serve.

General Tso's Shredded Chicken

[Servings: 4]

Ingredients:

- 10 Chicken Drumsticks
- 10 Dried Chinese Red Chili
- 2 stalks of Green Onion [Finely Chop Green Part for Garnish and Cut White Part into 1.5-Inch Pieces]
- 3 cloves of Minced Garlic
- 1 slice of Ginger [Roughly Chopped]
- 1 tbsp. Peanut Oil
- 1 tbsp. Honey [Optional]

General Tso's Sauce:

- ¼ cup Sugar
- ¼ cup Dark Soy Sauce
- 2 tbsp. Chinese Black Vinegar or Distilled White Vinegar
- 2 tbsp. Shaoxing Wine
- 1 tsp. Sesame Oil

Thickener:

- 2 tbsp. Cornstarch
- 2 tbsp. Water

Serve:

- 20 pieces of Lettuce
- Hoisin Sauce [Optional]

Directions:

1. Sauté garlic and ginger. On your Instant Pot press the Sauté button. While heating, pour in tbsp. peanut oil. Add dried Chinese red chili, minced garlic, white part of green onions and chopped ginger into your Instant Pot and allow them to slowly release their fragrance. Sauté for roughly approximately 3 minutes.
2. Add sauce mixture and chicken drumsticks into Instant Pot. Close the lid and pressure cook at High pressure for 12 minutes. Once done cooking Natural release for 12 minutes. Release the remaining pressure and open the lid carefully
3. Place chicken drumsticks in a large-sized mixing bowl. Remove chicken skin if desired. Shred the chicken drumsticks with a fork. Remove the bones
4. Remove the Chinese red chili. On your Instant Pot press the Sauté button and bring the sauce back to a boil. Taste sauce and add in honey to sweeten sauce if desired
5. Mix cornstarch with water and stir mixture into the sauce one third at a time until desired thickness. Place shredded chicken back into the sauce and mix together well. Place pulled chicken onto lettuce. Garnish with finely chopped green onion. You may add some Hoisin Sauce on the side. Serve.

Pot Roast

[Servings: 4]

Ingredients:

- 2 lbs. of Quartered Boneless Beef Chuck
- 3 cups of Chunked Onion
- 5 ⅓ cups of Chunked Carrot
- 6 cups of Peeled and Chunked Yukon Gold Potato
- 1 ounce of Dried Onion Soup Mix
- 2 cups Hot Water

Directions:

1. Add beef roast to Instant Pot. In bowl, mix together onion soup mix and hot water
2. Once dissolved, pour over beef. Add in vegetables. Lock cover into place and seal the steam nozzle. Manually set for approximately 25 minutes. Quick release pressure. Serve

Beef Rouladen

[Servings: 6]

Ingredients:

- 2 lbs. of Standing Boneless Rib Roast
- ½ cup Chopped Celery
- 1 cup Chopped Onion
- 2 cloves of Minced Garlic
- ½ cup Raisins
- 1 cup Seasoned Stove Top Stuffing
- ¼ cup Butter
- 2 tbsp. Water
- 1 tbsp. Tomato Puree
- 2 tsp. Powdered Beef Bouillon [Optional]
- 4 Carrots [Peeled and Cut into Pieces]
- 2 Bay Leaves
- 1 cup Beef Bouillon
- 1 tsp. Dried Thyme
- ¼ tsp. Salt
- ¼ tsp. Pepper
- Fresh Parsley [Optional]

Directions:

1. Cut roast into 6 equal slices [1-inch thickness each]. Heat up your Instant Pot on the sauté function. Melt ¼ cup butter add powdered beef bouillon and swish around a bit
2. Sauté ½ cup onion, garlic, celery, raisins, until onions are translucent and then add stove top stuffing and 2 tbsp. water. Season with salt and pepper. Add powdered beef bouillon if desired. Mix together well.
3. Divide mixture among pounded slices of beef. Mound stuffing at one end of each steakette and roll it up. You may tie it with a string or skewer it with small metal skewers to keep it rolled up.
4. Heat your Instant Pot again, heat oil and brown all of rolls. On top of browned rolls in your Instant Pot put in carrots, the other ½ cup onions, the cup liquid beef bouillon with 1 tbsp. tomato puree mixed into it, bay leaves, thyme and pepper.
5. Secure the lid on your Instant Pot using the Meat setting or manually set for approximately 15 minutes. Once finished, allow the pressure to naturally release.
6. When done place rolls on a plate, place carrots on top and remove the bay leaves. Heat your Instant Pot and thicken gravy by sprinkling flour over top, allowing it to soak in and stir. Pour some of gravy over the rolls and put the rest in a gravy boat. Sprinkle everything with fresh parsley if you so desire. Serve.

Cranberry Maple Orange Pork Chops

[Servings: 4]

Ingredients:

- 1 ⅓ lbs. of Pork Chops Bone-In
- 3 ½ cups of Peeled and Diced Sweet Potato
- ½ cup Orange Juice
- ⅓ cups of Fresh Cranberries
- ¼ cup Sliced Red Onion
- ¼ cup Maple Syrup
- 4 tbsp. Coconut Oil
- 2 tsp. Chopped Fresh Rosemary
- 1 ½ tsp. Cinnamon
- 1 tsp. Minced Garlic Cloves
- 1 tsp. Sea Salt

Directions:

1. Place pork chops in Instant Pot. Sear using Sauté function for approximately 2 minutes per side. Remove from Instant Pot. Melt coconut oil in Instant Pot. Add sweet potatoes and red onion. Sauté for approximately 10 minutes, or until potatoes are tender.
2. Combine orange juice, maple syrup and sea salt in bowl. Place pork chops in pot, on top of vegetables. Pour orange juice mixture over meat and vegetables. Sprinkle with cinnamon, garlic, cranberries and rosemary.
3. Lock the cover into place and seal the steam nozzle. Set on the Meat / Stew setting or manually set for approximately 15 minutes. Natural release pressure for about 5 minutes then Quick release any of the remaining pressure. Serve.

Arroz Con Pollo

[Servings: 8]

Ingredients:

- 12 Boneless Skinless Chicken Thighs

Marinade

- ¼ cup Olive Oil
- 3 cloves of Garlic [Roughly Chopped]
- 2 tsp. Ground Cumin
- 2 tbsp. Fresh Lime Juice
- 3 tbsp. Fresh Minced Oregano
- 1 tbsp. Sea Salt
- ½ tsp. Fresh Ground Black Pepper

Sofrito

- ½ Medium Green Bell Pepper [Seeded and Coarsely Chopped]
- ½ Medium Yellow Onion [Coarsely Chopped]
- 4 cloves of Garlic
- 1 handful of Cilantro
- ½ tsp. Sea Salt
- ¼ tsp. Fresh Ground Black Pepper

Rice

- 28-ounce can of Muir Glen Organic Fire Roasted Diced Tomatoes [With Liquid]
- 1 Medium Red Bell Pepper [Seeded and Diced]
- 1 Medium Yellow Onion [Diced]
- 1 ½ cups of Spanish Olives
- 3 cups of Long Grain Brown Rice
- 5 cups of Organic Chicken Stock
- 2 tbsp. Coconut Oil
- 2 tbsp. Olive Brine
- 1 tbsp. Minced Fresh Oregano
- 1 tsp. Ground Cumin
- ¼ tsp. Sea Salt

Directions:

1. Combine olive oil, pepper, garlic, sea salt, cumin, oregano and lime in a large-sized non-reactive bowl or zip top bag. Add chicken and coat evenly with marinade. Allow the marinade to sit for at least one hour up to overnight. Stir occasionally
2. Combine garlic, cilantro, onion, green bell pepper, pepper and sea salt in a food processor and process until smooth.
3. Heat the inner liner of your Instant Pot on the "Sauté" setting. Melt coconut oil. Remove chicken from the marinade, save any leftovers, brown chicken in batches for approximately 5 minutes on each side, until golden brown. Transfer chicken to a plate and set to the side
4. Add cumin, onion, red bell pepper and oregano. Sauté until just tender. Should take about 5 minutes. Stir in sofrito and sauté another 3 minutes. Add any leftover marinade, diced tomatoes, stock and sea salt. Simmer for approximately 2 minutes.
5. Stir in rice, brine and olives. Add browned chicken pieces to the pot. Place the lid on your Instant Pot and lock into place. Press the Meat / Stew Button; adjust the time so that the pressure time is at 15 minutes. When done and pressure has naturally released, remove lid. Serve

Awesome Sweet and Sour Spare Ribs

[Servings: 6]

Ingredients:

- 4 lbs. of Ribs [Trimmed and Cut for Serving]
- 20-ounce can of Pineapple
- ⅓ cup Rice Wine
- ⅓ cup Brown Sugar
- ¼ cup Ketchup
- 2 cloves of Chopped Garlic
- 1 Medium Onion [Sliced]
- ¼ tbsp. Soy Sauce
- 1 tsp. Finely Chopped Ginger
- 1 tbsp. Oil
- 1 tsp. Chili Powder
- 1 tsp. Fish Sauce [Optional]
- 1 tsp. Ground Coriander
- Pinch of Smoked Paprika
- Corn Starch Slurry
- Salt
- Pepper

Directions:

1. Add oil and sauté onions until translucent. Add the rest of ingredients except the cornstarch slurry. Make sure spareribs are submerged in sauce. You can marinate refrigerated in pot for several hours
2. Cook on the "Stew" setting for 12 minutes, leave on keep warm for approximately 3 minutes. Release the pressure. Check meat for doneness and moisture. If you need more time set timer to "Stew" for an additional 2 to 3 minutes
3. When meat is done, remove meat to a bowl and adjust the seasoning. Set to Sauté, when sauce starts to boil, add cornstarch slurry to thicken to desired taste and stir for 1 minute. Add the rice and vegetables of choice. Serve.

Ranch Pork Chops

[**Servings:** 4]

Ingredients:

- 2 lbs. of Boneless Pork Chops
- 1 ounce of Ranch Dressing Mix
- 10 ½ ounces of Cream of Chicken Soup
- 1 ¼ cup Water

Directions:

1. In Instant Pot, combine all of ingredients. Lock the cover into place and seal the steam nozzle
2. Set on the Meat / Stew setting and adjust to 15 minutes, or set manually for approximately 15 minutes. Quick release the pressure. Serve.

Jambalaya

[**Servings:** 10]

Ingredients:

- 1 lb. of Chicken Breasts and Thighs [Diced]
- 1 lb. of Andouille Sausage [Pre-Cooked and Sliced]
- 1 lb. of Prawns
- 1 ½ cups of Rice
- 1 cup Crushed Tomatoes
- 3 ½ cups of Chicken Stock
- 2 cups of Tri-Color Bell Peppers [Diced]
- 2 cups of Yellow Onions [Finely Diced]
- 2 tbsp. Olive Oil
- 2 tbsp. Minced Garlic
- 1 tbsp. Worcestershire Sauce
- 1 tbsp. + 1 tsp. Creole Seasoning

Directions:

1. Set your Instant Pot to "Sauté". Coat chicken with 1 tbsp. creole seasoning and brown the meat on all sides. Remove chicken from the heat and set to the side
2. Add onions, garlic, peppers and sauce until onions are translucent. Add rice and sauce for 2 minutes. Add tomato puree, creole seasoning, Worcestershire and chicken. Close the lid and press "Rice"
3. When rice is cooked, release the steam, remove the lid and add sausage and prawns. Place the lid back on Instant Pot, press "Manual" and cook an additional 2 minutes. Serve

Citrus Herb Chicken

[**Servings:** 4]

Ingredients:

- 2 ½ lbs. of Chicken Thighs Bone-In
- ½ cup Tangerine Juice
- ¼ cup Lemon Juice
- ¼ cup White Wine
- 2 tsp. Minced Garlic Cloves
- ¼ tsp. Dried Thyme
- 1 tsp. Fresh Chopped Rosemary
- 1/8 tsp. Salt
- 1/8 tsp. Black Pepper

Directions:

1. Place chicken thighs into Instant Pot. In bowl, combine lemon juice, wine, tangerine juice, garlic, thyme, rosemary, salt and pepper.
2. Pour sauce over chicken. Lock the cover into place and seal the steam nozzle
3. Set on the Poultry setting or set manually for approximately 15 minutes. Naturally release pressure for 5 minutes and Quick release any of the remaining pressure. Serve.

Country Steak

[Servings: 8]

Ingredients:

- 3 lbs. of Beef Round Steak
- ½ cup All-Purpose Flour
- ½ cup Diced Celery
- ½ cup Diced Onion
- 2 cups of Kettle and Fire's Beef Bone Broth
- ½ cup Ketchup
- 6 cloves of Garlic [Medium-Sized]
- 2 tbsp. Vegetable Oil
- 1 tbsp. Worcestershire Sauce
- 1 tsp. Salt
- ¼ tsp. Black Pepper

Directions:

1. Cut steak into equal portions. Pat the flour onto both sides of steak. Heat vegetable oil in your Instant Pot using the Sauté function.
2. In batches, brown steaks on both sides. Add remaining ingredients to Instant Pot. Lock the lid in place and seal the steam nozzle.
3. Select the Meat / Stew setting and adjust to 30 minutes, or set manually for 30 minutes. Natural release for about 5 minutes then Quick release any of the remaining pressure. Serve.

Carnitas

[Servings: 8]

Ingredients:

- 3 lbs. of Quartered Pork Roast
- 4 ounces of Canned Diced Mild Green Chiles
- ½ cup Chicken Broth / Stock
- 1 cup Medium Salsa
- ½ cup Tequila
- 1 ½ cups of Fresh Cilantro
- 3 tsp. Minced Garlic Cloves
- ½ tsp. Salt
- ½ tsp. Black Pepper

Directions:

1. Trim pork roast of excess fat and cut in half. Place in Instant Pot. Top with garlic, salt and pepper
2. Add in the remaining ingredients to Instant Pot. Lock the lid and seal the steam nozzle. Cook on Manual for approximately 50 minutes
3. Naturally release the pressure for 10 minutes. Quick release any of the remaining pressure. Remove lid and shred the pork. Serve.

Orange Adobo Chicken

[Servings: 4]

Ingredients:

- 2 lbs. of Quartered Chicken Boneless Breasts
- 1 cup Orange Juice
- ¼ cup Brown Sugar
- 2 tbsp. Minced Chipotle Peppers in Adobo Sauce
- 1 tbsp. Season Salt
- ½ tsp. Black Pepper
- ½ tsp. Salt

Directions:

1. In Instant Pot, heat orange juice and brown sugar using the Sauté function until sugar dissolves. Whisk in season salt, salt, pepper, chipotle peppers and cook for approximately 3 to 4 minutes
2. Add chicken breasts, then turn to cover well with sauce. Lock the lid in place and seal the steam vent.

3. Select the Poultry setting and adjust to 10 minutes or set manually for approximately 10 minutes. Natural release for 5 minutes then Quick release any of the remaining pressure. Serve

Spiced Cranberry Pot Roast

[**Servings:** 6]

Ingredients:

- 4 lbs. of Beef Arm Roast
- 1 cup Whole Cranberries [Fresh or Frozen]
- ½ cup White Wine
- ¼ cup Honey
- ½ cup Water
- 2 cloves of Garlic [Peeled But Left Whole]
- 2 cups of Bone Broth
- 2 tbsp. Olive Oil
- 3-Inch Cinnamon Stick
- 1 tsp. Horseradish Powder
- 6 Whole Cloves
- Salt
- Pepper

Directions:

1. Pat meat dry with paper towels and season generously with salt and pepper. Press the Sauté button on your Instant Pot and heat oil until shimmering. Brown roast on all sides. Should take 8 to 10 minutes total. Remove and set to the side
2. Pour wine into empty pot and use wooden spoon to scrape up brown bits. Allow it to cook for approximately 4 to 5 minutes, stirring constantly to deglaze pot. Add cranberries, honey, water, horseradish powder, garlic, cinnamon stick and whole cloves. Cook for approximately 4 to 5 minutes, stirring constantly, or until cranberries start to burst
3. Return meat to pot, nestling it into cranberries. Add enough bone broth to bring liquid level to nearly covering meat.
4. Lock the lid in place. Program your Instant Pot to cook under High pressure for approximately 75 minutes. Turn your Instant Pot off immediately after 75 minutes and allow the pressure to release naturally for about 15 minutes. Quick release any of the remaining pressure
5. Transfer meat to serving platter and pour some of the cranberry sauce over top. Reserve the rest of cooking juice to pass at the table. Serve.

Duck with Vegetables

[**Servings:** 8]

Ingredients:

- 1 Cucumber [Cut into Pieces]
- 1 Medium Duck
- 1 small piece of Ginger [Cut into Pieces]
- 2 Carrots [Cut into Pieces]
- 2 cups of water
- 1 tbsp. Cooking Wine
- 2 tsp. Salt

Directions:

1. Put all of ingredients into Instant Pot. Press the Meat / Stew button. Remove from your Instant Pot once finished cooking. Serve

Brown Sugar Garlic Chicken

[Servings: 4]

Ingredients:

- 1 lb. of Quartered Chicken Boneless Breasts
- ⅓ cup Brown Sugar
- ¼ cup Lemon Lime Soda
- ⅓ cup Vinegar
- 2 tbsp. Gluten-Free Soy Sauce
- 2 tsp. Minced Garlic Cloves
- 1 tsp. Black Pepper

Directions:

1. Place all of ingredients into Instant Pot. Lock the cover into place and seal the steam nozzle.
2. Set on the Poultry setting or manually set for approximately 15 minutes. Naturally release pressure for about 5 minutes and Quick release any of the remaining pressure. Serve

Cherry Apple Pork Loin

[Servings: 4]

Ingredients:

- 1 ⅓ lbs. of Quartered Boneless Pork Loin
- ½ cup Apple Juice
- ⅓ cup Diced Onion
- ⅓ cup Diced Celery
- 2 cups of Diced Apple
- ⅔ cup Pitted Cherry
- ½ cup Water
- 1/8 tsp. Salt
- 1/8 tsp. Black Pepper

Directions:

1. Place pork, water, apple juice, salt and pepper in Instant Pot. Lock the lid into place and seal the steam nozzle. Cook on the Meat / Stew setting and set the timer for approximately 30 minutes
2. Natural release for 5 minutes then Quick release any of the remaining pressure. Add in remaining ingredients. Lock the lid in place. Manually set for 3 minutes. Quick release the pressure. Serve.

Bourbon Honey Chicken

[Servings: 4]

Ingredients:

- 1 ½ lbs. of Chicken Thighs [Boneless and Skinless]
- ½ cup Soy Sauce
- ¼ cup Ketchup
- ½ cup Diced Onion
- 1 cup Honey
- 2 tsp. Minced Garlic Cloves
- 2 tbsp. Vegetable Oil
- ¼ tbsp. Red Pepper Flakes
- 1/8 tsp. Salt
- 1/8 tsp. Black Pepper

Directions:

1. Place all ingredients except for cornstarch and water into Instant Pot. Lock the cover into place and seal the steam nozzle
2. Cook on the Chicken setting or manually set for approximately 15 minutes. If you are using frozen chicken, add an additional 10 minutes. Naturally release pressure for about 5 minutes then Quick release any of the remaining pressure.
3. Remove chicken and dice. Set the Instant Pot setting to Sauté. In bowl, combine cornstarch and water. Add cornstarch mixture and chicken to pot and continue to cook for 2 to 3 minutes until thickened. Serve.

Creamy Italian Chicken Recipe

[**Servings:** 4]

Ingredients:

- 2 lbs. of Quartered Chicken Boneless Breasts
- 8 ounces of Softened Cream Cheese
- 3 cups of Cream of Chicken Soup
- 8 cups of Farfalle [Bowtie]
- 2 cups of Water
- 2 tbsp. Italian Dressing Dry Mix

Directions:

1. If chicken breasts are larger than 1/4-inch thick, cut them in half lengthwise to reduce the thickness.
2. In Instant Pot, mix together chicken, cream cheese, dressing mix, cream of chicken soup and water. Lock the cover into place and seal the steam nozzle
3. Cook on the Chicken setting or manually set for approximately 15 minutes. If you are using a frozen chicken, add an additional 10 minutes. Naturally release pressure for about 5 minutes then quick release any of the remaining pressure. Serve.

Cream Cheese Chicken

[**Servings:** 6]

Ingredients:

- 2 lbs. of Quartered Chicken Boneless Breasts
- 8 ounces of Cream Cheese [Fat-Free]
- 10 ¾ ounces of Cream of Chicken Soup [Fat-Free]
- 1 ounce of Italian Dressing Dry Mix

Directions:

1. Place chicken breasts, cream cheese, soup, cream and dressing mix into Instant Pot
2. Lock the cover into place and seal the steam nozzle. Set on the Poultry setting or manually set for approximately 15 minutes. Naturally release pressure for about 5 minutes then quick release any of the remaining pressure. Serve.

Shrimp and Pork Dumplings

[**Servings:** 24]

Ingredients:

Shrimp Paste

- ½ lb. of Shrimps [Finely Chopped]
- ¼ tsp. Salt
- 1 tsp. Cornstarch
- ½ tsp. Oil [Optional]

Pork Paste

- ½ lb. of Ground Pork
- 1 tbsp. Shaoxing Wine
- 1 tbsp. Cornstarch
- 2 tbsp. Unsalted Chicken Stock
- ½ tsp. Ground White Pepper
- 2 tsp. Light Soy Sauce
- 1 tsp. Sesame Oil
- 1 tsp. Fish Sauce
- ½ tsp. Sugar

Other

- 2 slices of Grated Ginger
- 24 Round Wonton Wrappers
- ¾ stalk of Green Onions [Finely Chopped]
- 2 Dried Shiitake Mushrooms [Re-Hydrated and Finely Chopped]

Directions:

1. Pat dry shrimps with paper towels. Place chopped shrimps in a medium-sized mixing bowl. Add in 1 tsp. cornstarch and ¼ tsp. salt. Place ground pork in a large-sized mixing bowl. Pour in 1 tbsp. cornstarch, ground white pepper, sugar, Shaoxing wine, light soy sauce, fish sauce, sesame oil and unsalted chicken stock.
2. Squeeze and mix seasoned ground pork with hands, then throw it against mixing bowl until it resembles a paste-like consistency
3. Wash hands and do the same with seasoned shrimps. Put pastes into fridge and prepare remaining ingredients. Finely chop stalk of green onions and pieces of re-hydrated Shiitake mushrooms. Use a grater to grate 2 ginger slices.
4. Remove pork and shrimp pastes from fridge. Pour all of ingredients into ground pork paste mixing bowl. Squeeze and mix ingredients with hands until blended. Remember to throw the paste against mixing bowl.
5. Place a Wonton wrapper on one hand. Scoop roughly 1 tbsp. mixed paste on Wonton wrapper with butter knife or the dull end of spoon
6. Then, wrap it into a cylinder shape with an open top. Place parchment liner into bamboo steamer, then place mixture on the liner. Close bamboo steamer lid.
7. Cook in Instant Pot. Place steamer rack and pour one cup water into Instant Pot. Place bamboo steamer filled with mixture into Instant Pot. Close lid and cook at High pressure for 3 minutes. Wait for about 5 minutes and do a Quick release. Remove the bamboo steamer from pot. Serve

Honey Chicken

[Servings: 4]

Ingredients:

- 2 lbs. of Boneless Pork Chops
- ¼ cup Honey
- ½ tbsp. Maple Syrup
- 2 tbsp. Dijon Mustard
- ½ tsp. Peeled and Minced Fresh Ginger
- ¼ tsp. Ground Cloves
- ½ tsp. Cinnamon
- ½ tsp. Sea Salt
- ¼ tsp. Black Pepper

Directions:

1. Sprinkle pork chops with salt and pepper and place in Instant Pot. Set your Instant Pot to Sauté. Brown pork chops on each side
2. In bowl, combine honey, Dijon mustard, ginger, maple syrup, cloves and cinnamon.
3. Pour over pork chops. Lock the cover into place and seal the steam nozzle
4. Set on the Manual setting for approximately 15 minutes. Naturally release pressure for 5 minutes and Quick release any of the remaining pressure. Serve.

Beer Potato Fish

[Servings: 6]

Ingredients:

- 1 lb. of Fish Fillet
- 4 Medium Potatoes [Peeled and Diced]
- 1 cup Beer
- 1 Sliced Red Pepper
- 1 tbsp. Rock Candy
- 1 tbsp. Oyster Flavored Sauce
- 1 tbsp. Oil
- 1 tsp. Salt

Directions:

1. Put all of ingredients into Instant Pot. Press the Bean / Chili setting. Should take about 40 minutes. Allow the pressure to release naturally. Once finished remove from Instant Pot. Serve

Honey Glazed Chicken Thighs

[**Servings:** 6]

Ingredients:

- 1 ¼ lbs. of Chicken Thighs Boneless and Skinless
- ½ cup Honey
- ½ cup Water
- 2 tbsp. Apple Cider Vinegar
- 1 tsp. Chili Powder
- 1 tsp. Red Pepper Flakes
- 2 tsp. Garlic Powder
- 2 tsp. Paprika
- 1 tsp. Kosher Salt
- 1 tsp. Black Pepper

Directions:

1. Mix together salt, pepper, chili powder, red pepper flakes, garlic powder and paprika set to the side. Mix water, honey and cider vinegar. Set to the side. Position chicken thighs so they lie flat
2. Cover all sides in seasoning and place the chicken in Instant Pot. Pour honey mixture over chicken. Lock lid in place and seal the steam nozzle.
4. Select the Poultry setting and adjust to 12 minutes, or set manually to approximately 12 minutes. Natural release for 5 minutes then Quick release any of the remaining pressure. Keep chicken with all the excess glaze. Serve.

Barbeque Hawaiian Turkey Meatloaf

[**Servings:** 6]

Ingredients:

- 2 lbs. of Ground Turkey
- 15-ounce can of Diced Tomatoes
- 1 Red Pepper [Finely Chopped]
- 1 Medium Onion [Minced]
- 3 cloves of Garlic [Minced]
- 1 cup Crushed Pineapple [Drained]
- ½ cup Dry Red Wine
- 1 ½ cups of Whole Grain Bread [Cubed]
- 2 Eggs
- 1 ½ tbsp. Worcestershire Sauce
- 2 tbsp. Olive Oil
- 3 ½ tbsp. Sour Cream or Creme Fraiche
- 1 tbsp. Soy Sauce
- 3 tbsp. BBQ Sauce
- 3 tbsp. Ketchup
- Pinch of Cayenne Pepper
- 1 tsp. Parsley [Fresh or Dried]
- 1 tsp. Paprika
- 1 tsp. Sea Salt
- ½ tsp. Freshly Ground Black Pepper

Directions:

1. In skillet, put in 1 tbsp. olive oil and add you red pepper, garlic and onions. Sauté until onions are almost transparent. Add chopped tomatoes and cook down until almost all of the fluid has been cooked out of it. Set to the side to cool
2. In skillet, add 1 tbsp. olive oil, bread cubes and a pinch of the salt, pepper, parsley, cayenne and paprika to olive oil. Sauté until bread cubes are well toasted.
3. In a mixing bowl add ground turkey, sour cream, eggs, Worcestershire sauce, wine and soy sauce. Mix together well
4. Add cooled seasoned mixture to turkey mixture. Add loaf into ceramic or glass dish. Use a loaf pan that will fit inside Instant Pot
5. Top with mixture of ketchup and BBQ sauce. Sprinkle pineapple over top of sauces. Foil the top of turkey meatloaf to seal it and keep it moist
6. Add 2 cups of water to the inside pan in Instant Pot. Set in trivet. Add in turkey meatloaf on top of trivet. Set your Instant Pot to the "Meat" setting. Once done, allow your Instant Pot to cool down naturally for at least 10 minutes. Slice meatloaf. Serve.

Roast Chicken

[**Servings:** 4]

Ingredients:

- 5 lbs. of Whole Chicken
- 1 tbsp. Olive Oil
- 1 tbsp. Herbs de Provence
- 1 tsp. Minced Garlic Cloves
- 1 tsp. Lemon [Juiced]
- 1 tsp. Lemon [Zested]
- 1 cup Chicken Broth / Stock
- 1 tsp. Salt
- ½ tsp. Black Pepper

Directions:

1. Mix all ingredients together, except the chicken, in a bowl. Set spice mixture to the side. Turn chicken breast side down. Using sharp kitchen shears, cut along both sides of the backbone of chicken, cutting through the ribs.
2. Remove the backbone and save for stock. [If there are giblets, remove those too. Discard or save for another use]. Turn chicken back over and pull back the breasts [you will hear some bones crack] so that it lays completely flat, including the legs.
3. Using sharp knife, cut a slit near the breast and on each leg so that you can reach hand inside [do not remove skin]. Rub spice mixture all over the meat by sliding hand underneath the skin. Reserve just a little bit to rub on the outside of the skin
4. Add chicken and chicken broth to Instant Pot. Cook on the Poultry setting for approximately 32 minutes or for 6 minutes per pound plus 2 additional minutes. Release pressure naturally. Serve.

Coconut Chicken Curry

[**Servings:** 4]

Ingredients:

- 3 ¾ cups of Diced Chicken Boneless Breasts
- 10 fluid ounces of Canned Coconut Milk
- 3 cups of Chunked Green Bell Pepper
- 8 ounces of Tomato Paste
- 2 Onions [Halved]
- 2 tsp. Minced Garlic Cloves
- 1 tbsp. Curry Powder
- 1 tbsp. Garam Masala
- 2 tbsp. Almond Butter
- 1 ½ tsp. Salt

Directions:

1. Blend all ingredients except for chicken in food processor. Place chicken in Instant Pot. Pour sauce over. Lock the lid in place and seal the steam nozzle.
2. Select the Poultry setting and adjust to 9 minutes or manually set for approximately 9 minutes. Naturally release the pressure for 5 minutes, then Quick release any of the remaining pressure. Serve.

Herb Buttermilk Chicken

[Servings: 4]

Ingredients:

- 2 lbs. of Quartered Chicken Boneless Breasts
- 1 cup Buttermilk
- 1 tbsp. Dijon Mustard
- 1 tbsp. Honey
- 1 tbsp. Dried Rosemary
- 1 tsp. Dried Thyme
- 1 tsp. Dried Sage
- 1 tsp. Black Pepper
- 1 tsp. Salt

Directions:

1. Place all of ingredients into freezer bag. Allow to marinate in refrigerator for at least 1 hour. Place chicken breasts and marinade into Instant Pot. Lock the cover into place and seal the steam nozzle.
2. Set on the Poultry setting or manually for approximately 15 minutes. Naturally release pressure for 5 minutes then Quick release any of the remaining pressure. Serve.

Harvest Ham Dinner

[Servings: 2]

Ingredients:

- 1 Ham [Sliced 3/4-Inch Thick]
- 1 can of Sliced Pineapple
- ½ cup Brown Sugar [Firmly Packed]
- ½ cup Pineapple Juice
- 3 Sweet Potatoes [Peeled and Cubed]
- Frozen Pierogies [Potato]
- 1 tbsp. Cooking Oil
- ½ tsp. Ground Cloves
- Sour Cream

Directions:

1. Heat oil in your Instant Pot on the Sauté function. Add slices of ham. Add pineapple juice and use the Manual mode to pressure cook for approximately 5 minutes.
2. Reduce the pressure manually by turning the steam release to Venting. Add sweet potatoes and pineapple. Sprinkle with brown sugar and add cloves. Arrange frozen pierogies on top
3. Use the Manual mode to pressure cook for approximately 7 minutes. Release pressure and remove from cooker.. Garnish with a dollop of sour cream. Serve.

Coconut Tofu Curry

[Servings: 4]

Ingredients:

- 10 fluid ounces of Canned Light Coconut Milk
- 8 ounces of Tomato Paste
- 1 cup Chunked Onion
- 1 cup Diced Tofu [Firm]
- 1 tbsp. Curry Powder
- 2 cups of Chunked Green Bell Pepper
- 1 tbsp. Garam Masala
- 2 tbsp. Creamy Peanut Butter
- 2 tsp. Minced Garlic Cloves
- 1 ½ tsp. Sea Salt

Directions:

1. Blend all of ingredients except tofu in a food processor. Place tofu in Instant Pot. Pour sauce over. Lock the lid in place and seal the steam nozzle
2. Cook on Manual for approximately 4 minutes. Quick release the pressure. Serve.

Braised Duck with Potato

[Servings: 4]

Ingredients:

- 1 Whole Duck [Chopped into Chunks]
- 2 Green Onions [Cut into 2-Inches Length]
- Sliced Fresh Ginger Root [1-Inch Piece]
- 1 Potato [Chopped into Cubes]
- 4 cloves of Garlic
- ¼ cup Water
- 4 tbsp. Soy Sauce
- 4 tbsp. Sugar
- 4 tbsp. Rice / Sherry Wine
- ½ tsp. Salt

Directions:

1. Heat up your Instant Pot by pressing "Sauté" setting for approximately 1 minute. Sear chopped duck in your Instant Pot with skin side down until golden brown
2. Stir in and mix all of ingredients into Instant Pot, except potato and press "Poultry." After poultry cycle, release the pressure and open lid. Stir in potato cubes and press "Manual" for another 5 minutes. Serve.

Maple Mustard Chicken

[Servings: 6]

Ingredients:

- 2 lbs. of Quartered Chicken Boneless Breasts
- ½ cup Maple Syrup
- ⅓ cup Stone Ground Mustard
- ½ cups of Water
- 2 tbsp. Quick Tapioca

Directions:

1. Place chicken into Instant Pot. In bowl, combine maple syrup, tapioca, mustard and water. Pour over chicken.
2. Lock the lid into place and seal the steam nozzle. Select the Poultry setting and adjust to 10 minutes or manually set to 10 minutes. Natural release for about 5 minutes then Quick release any of the remaining pressure. Serve

Chicken Parmigiana

[Servings: 12]

Ingredients:

- 3 lbs. of Quartered Chicken Boneless Breasts
- 48 ounces of Tomato Sauce
- 4 cups of Shredded Mozzarella Cheese
- 1 cup Olive Oil
- 1 cup Grated Parmesan Cheese
- 4 tbsp. Salted Butter
- ½ tsp. Garlic Powder

Directions:

1. Heat oil in your Instant Pot on the Sauté setting. Quickly brown each piece of chicken on both sides. Add Parmesan cheese, garlic powder, butter and tomato sauce on top of chicken. Lock the lid into place and seal the steam nozzle
5. Cook on the Poultry setting or manual setting for approximately 15 minutes. Quick release the pressure. Sprinkle with mozzarella cheese, replace cover and allow to melt for approximately 5 minutes. Serve.

Soups, Sides and Snacks Recipes

Mexican Style Chicken Soup

[Servings: 6]

Ingredients:

- 4 cups of Cooked and Diced Chicken Boneless Breasts
- ⅔ cup Diced Red Onion
- 1 ¾ cups of Tomato Juice
- 1 cup Avocado
- ¼ cup Seeded and Diced Jalapeño
- 1 ½ cups of Diced Carrot
- ½ cup Diced Roma Tomato
- ½ cup Chopped Fresh Cilantro
- 6 cups of Chicken Broth / Stock
- 4 tsp. Minced Garlic Cloves
- 2 tsp. Sea Salt
- 1 tsp. Ground Coriander
- 1 tbsp. Cumin
- 1 tbsp. Chili Powder
- 2 tbsp. Lime [Juiced]

Directions:

1. Place all of ingredients in your Instant Pot except the avocado. Lock the lid into place and seal the steam nozzle. Choose the Soup setting and adjust to 10 minutes or set manually for approximately 10 minutes
2. Allow the pressure to release naturally for 5 minutes then release any of the remaining pressure. Add sliced avocado on top. Serve.

Chorizo Chili

[Servings: 6]

Ingredients:

- ¾ cups of Cooked Ground Chorizo Sausage
- 15 ounces of Drained Canned Whole Kernel Corn
- 16 ounces of Salsa Verde
- 15 ounces of Canned Diced Tomatoes
- 1 ½ cups of Drained and Rinsed Great Northern Beans [Canned]
- 30 ounces of Drained and Rinsed Black Beans [Canned]
- 1 tsp. Chili Powder
- 1 tsp. Minced Garlic Cloves
- 1 tsp. Cumin
- 1 cup Cold Water

Directions:

1. Remove the casing from chorizo. Place chorizo in your Instant Pot and saute until fully cooked. Add remaining ingredients. Lock the cover into place and seal the steam nozzle
2. Cook on the Bean / Chili setting or manual for approximately 30 minutes. Quick release the pressure. Allow it to sit for 10 minutes with the lid off before serving. Serve.

Curried Coconut Chicken Soup

[**Servings:** 8]

Ingredients:

- 3 cups of Cooked and Diced Chicken Bone-In Breasts
- ¼ cup Fresh Cilantro
- 2 cups of Diced Onion
- 2 cups of Sliced Carrot
- 2 cups of Basmati Rice
- 4 cups of Chicken Broth / Stock
- 1 ¾ cups of Canned Coconut Milk
- 3 cups of Sliced Red Bell Pepper
- 2 tbsp. Soy Sauce
- 1 tbsp. Curry Powder
- 2 tbsp. Olive Oil
- 1 tbsp. Peeled and Minced Fresh Ginger
- 1 ½ tbsp. Chopped Lemongrass
- 2 tbsp. Sriracha Sauce
- 2 tbsp. Creamy Peanut Butter
- 8 individual Lime
- 4 tsp. Minced Garlic Cloves
- 1 tsp. Sucanat
- 1 tsp. Salt

Directions:

1. Heat olive oil in your Instant Pot on the Sauté function. Sauté onions, carrots and pepper for about 3 to 4 minutes until they begin to soften.
2. Add garlic, curry powder and ginger and cook for 1 to 2 more minutes until fragrant. Pour in broth, lemongrass and salt. Bring to a boil and add chicken to Instant Pot.
3. Mix coconut milk, soy sauce, peanut butter, Sriracha and sucanat in bowl and add to soup. Lock lid in place and seal the steam nozzle.
4. Cook on Manual for approximately 3 minutes. Let the pressure release naturally for 5 minutes then release any of the remaining pressure. Stir in cilantro. Add hot cooked rice and garnish with lime wedges. Serve.

Tomato Basil and Beef Soup

[**Servings:** 4]

Ingredients:

- 1 ½ cups of Cooked Ground Beef
- 30 ounces of Canned Diced Tomatoes
- 1 cup Diced Onion
- 1 cup Canned Coconut Milk
- 1 cup Chicken Broth / Stock
- ¼ cups of Fresh Basil
- 1 tbsp. Coconut Oil
- 3 tsp. Minced Garlic Cloves
- 1 tsp. Salt

Directions:

1. Add diced tomatoes and coconut milk to blender and blend until smooth. Set your Instant Pot to Sauté and add coconut oil and onions. Cook until onions are translucent. Add garlic and cook until fragrant
2. Pour in tomato/coconut milk mixture, salt and chicken broth. Lock the lid into place and seal steam nozzle. Cook on Manual for approximately 10 minutes. Release the pressure manually. Mix in fresh basil and cooked ground beef. Hit cancel, then saute and cook until heated through. Serve.

Hamburger Barley Vegetable Soup

[Servings: 8]

Ingredients:

- 1 lb. of Hamburger
- 28-ounce can of Petite Tomatoes Undrained
- 2 Carrots [Peeled and Cut into 1/2-Inch Thick Slices]
- 2 Medium Potatoes [Peeled and Diced]
- ½ cup Chopped Onion
- 6 cups of Beef Broth
- 4 cups of Chopped Cabbage
- 1 cup Quick Barley
- ¼ cup Chopped Celery
- 12-ounce bag of Frozen Mixed Vegetables
- ½ tsp. Dried Basil
- 1 tsp. Minced Garlic
- ¼ tsp. Salt
- ¼ tsp. Pepper

Directions:

1. Sauté hamburger until no longer pink. Drain off the fat, add onion and saute until translucent. Add garlic and saute for 1 minute
2. Add tomatoes, beef broth and barley. Cook on High pressure using the Soup setting. Adjust to 10 minutes. Do a Quick pressure release then add the rest of vegetables and spices
3. Put lid back on and bring to High pressure using the Soup setting. Adjust to 15 minutes longer. Quick release the pressure. Serve.

Jalapeno Popper Chicken Chili

[Servings: 4]

Ingredients:

- 3 ⅓ cups of Cooked and Diced Chicken Boneless Breasts
- 14 ounces of Canned Whole Kernel Corn
- 10 ounces of Diced Tomatoes with Green Chiles
- 2 cups of Chicken Broth / Stock
- ⅔ cups of Seeded and Diced Jalapeño
- 1 cup Cooked and Diced Bacon
- 1 ¼ cups of Diced Onion
- 3 tsp. Minced Garlic Cloves
- 1 tsp. Cumin
- 2 tsp. Chili Powder
- 1 tsp. Dried Oregano
- 1/8 tsp. Salt
- ¼ tsp. Black Pepper

Directions:

1. Combine onions, jalapeno, chicken, garlic, cumin, chili powder, oregano, salt, black pepper, diced tomatoes, chicken broth and corn in Instant Pot
2. Lock the cover into place and seal the steam nozzle. Choose the Soup setting and adjust to 10 minutes or set manually for approximately 10 minutes.
3. Release the pressure naturally. Set on warm and stir in cream cheese and half of bacon and cook for approximately 3 minutes. Top with cheese, chips and the remaining half of bacon. Serve.

Split Pea with Ham Soup

[Servings: 4]

Ingredients:
- 2 cups of Dried Peas
- ½ cup Diced Ham
- 5 cups of Water
- 1 ½ tsp. Salt
- 1 tsp. Onion

Directions:
1. Cook in your Instant Pot for approximately 17 minutes on the "Manual" setting. Natural release the pressure when done. Once finished remove from pot. Serve

Creamy Tomato Soup

[Servings: 6]

Ingredients:
- 28-ounce can of Whole Peeled Tomatoes
- 28-ounce can of Crushed Tomatoes
- 2 Vegetarian Bouillon Cubes
- 4 cloves of Garlic
- 3 cups of Water
- ½ cup Cashew Pieces
- 3 tbsp. Oats [Rolled; Steel-Cut, or Scottish]
- 1 tbsp. Agave Nectar [Optional]
- 1 tbsp. Dried Basil
- Salt
- Pepper

Directions:
1. Add all of ingredients except for agave nectar, pepper and salt to Instant Pot. Cook on Manual for approximately 5 minutes and let the pressure come down naturally - that will take around 10 minutes
2. Carefully pour cooked mixture into a blender and blend until smooth. You may need to do this in 2 separate batches. Add agave nectar if using and salt and pepper to taste. You can also add more water if the soup is thicker than you want it to be. Serve.

African Style Chickpea Coconut Soup

[Servings: 4]

Ingredients:
- 15 ounces of Rinsed and Drained Canned Garbanzo Beans [Chick Peas]
- 14 ounces of Diced Fire Roasted Tomatoes
- 4 ounces of Canned Diced Mild Green Chiles
- 1 ½ cups of Peeled and Diced Apple [Granny Smith]
- 13 ½ fluid ounces of Canned Coconut Milk
- 3 cups of Vegetable Broth / Stock
- ⅔ cups of Peeled and Diced Sweet Potato
- ½ cup Cooked Quinoa
- 1 ½ cups of Diced Red Bell Pepper
- 2 tbsp. Dried Cilantro
- 1 tbsp. Green Curry Paste
- 1 tbsp. Lime [Juiced]
- 4 tsp. Diced Garlic Cloves
- ½ tsp. Cumin
- ½ tsp. Cinnamon
- 1 tsp. Sea Salt
- ½ tsp. Black Pepper

Directions:
1. Place all of ingredients in Instant Pot. Lock lid into place and seal the steam nozzle
2. Choose the Soup setting and adjust to 10 minutes or set manually for approximately 10 minutes. Let the pressure release naturally for 5 minutes then release any of the remaining pressure. Serve.

Sweet and Spicy Red Beans

[**Servings:** 4]

Ingredients:

- 10-ounce bag of Small Red Beans
- 1 Large Crisp Apple [Peeled and Chopped in 1-Inch Squares]
- ¼ cup Dark Brown Sugar
- 2 dashes of Cumin Powder
- 4 cloves of Minced Garlic
- 1 Small Yellow Onion [Finely Chopped]
- 4 dashes of Cayenne Pepper
- 10 tbsp. Ketchup
- 3 tbsp. Dry Oregano
- 1 tbsp. Sea Salt
- 12 twists of Fresh Black Pepper
- 1 dash of Celery Salt

Directions:

1. Soak beans overnight. Place soaked beans and ingredients in Instant Pot. Add fresh water with 2-inches over top of beans. Pressure cook for approximately 45 minutes. Allow it to cool naturally. Serve.

White Bean Chili Chicken

[**Servings:** 8]

Ingredients:

- 3 ¾ cups of Diced Chicken Boneless Breasts
- 14 ounces of Diced Tomatoes [Canned]
- 4 ounces of Diced Mild Green Chiles [Canned]
- 3 cups of Drained and Rinsed Great Northern Beans [Canned]
- 2 cups of Chicken Broth / Stock [Reduced Fat]
- 1 ¼ cups of Diced Onion
- 1 tbsp. Cumin
- ½ tsp. Paprika
- ¼ tsp. Cayenne Pepper
- ½ tsp. Garlic Powder

Directions:

1. Combine all of ingredients into Instant Pot. Lock the cover into place and seal the steam nozzle
2. Choose the Soup setting and adjust to 10 minutes or set manually for approximately 10 minutes. Release the pressure naturally. Serve

Hearty Beef Stew

[**Servings:** 8]

Ingredients:

- 2 lbs. of Stew Beef
- 14 ½ ounces of Canned Diced Tomatoes
- 1 whole Bay Leaf
- 14 fluid ounces of Kettle and Fire's Beef Bone Broth
- 2 cups of Diced Celery
- 3 cups of Diced Carrot
- 1 ½ cups of Diced Onion
- 4 cups of Peeled and Diced Russet Potato
- 3 tsp. Minced Garlic Cloves
- 1 tsp. Dried Basil
- 4 ½ tsp. Worcestershire Sauce
- 1 tsp. Dried Thyme
- ½ tsp. Black Pepper
- 1/8 tsp. Salt

Directions:

1. Place all of ingredients into Instant Pot. Lock the cover into place and seal the steam nozzle. Choose the Meat / Stew button and adjust to 35 minutes or set manually for approximately 35 minutes
2. Naturally release the pressure for 5 minutes and Quick release any of the remaining pressure. Remove the bay leaf. Serve.

Beef and Porcini Mushroom Stew

[**Servings:** 6]

Ingredients:

- 2 lbs. of Beef Chuck [Cut into 1-Inch Cubes]
- ½ cup Red Wine
- 1 cup Salt-Free Beef Stock
- 2 Large Carrots [Sliced into 1/2-Inch Rounds]
- 1 ounce of Dried Porcini Mushrooms [Rinsed]
- 1 stalk of Celery [Cut into 1/2-Inch Slices]
- 1 Medium Red Onion [Diced]
- 1 sprig of Rosemary [De-Stemmed and Finely Chopped]
- 1 tbsp. Olive Oil
- 2 tbsp. All-Purpose Flour
- 2 tbsp. Unsalted Butter
- 1 tsp. Salt
- ¼ tsp. pepper

Directions:

1. Set your Instant Pot on Sauté mode. Add olive oil and sear beef cubes on one side. Should take about 5 minutes. Add rosemary, celery, onions, red wine, stock, salt and pepper. Mix contents of the Instant Pot together well. Sprinkle the mushrooms and carrots on top of stew mixture
2. Close lid and cook for about 15 minutes at High pressure. When time is up, open your Instant Pot with Natural release. Should take about 15 to 20 minutes
3. In small-sized pan melt butter and drizzle with flour. Mix into a paste and allow it to cook until butter begins to make bubbles in flour.
4. Remove lid, tilting it away from you. Add about 6 tbsp. cooking liquid from your Instant Pot into small-sized pan with the flour paste and mix well to loosen paste. Pour mixture back into the Instant Pot and mix together well. Bring the contents of your Instant Pot to a boil by pressing Sauté mode and let it simmer until thickened. Should take about 5 minutes. Serve

Lentil Vegetable Soup

[**Servings:** 6]

Ingredients:

Sauté:

- 1 Minced Small Onion
- 1 clove of Minced Garlic
- 1 tbsp. Olive Oil

Soup:

- 1 Medium Potato [Peeled and Cubed]
- 1 Small Sweet Potato [Peeled and Cubed]
- 2 Medium Carrots [Cubed]
- 1 cup Lentil Blend
- 5 cups of Water
- 1 Bay Leaf
- 1 tsp. Marjoram
- 1 tsp. Thyme
- ¼ tsp. Rosemary Powder
- ½ tsp. Smoked Paprika

Finish:

- ¼ cup Nutritional Yeast
- Salt
- Pepper

Directions:

1. Turn on your Instant Pot and use the Sauté function. Heat olive oil, then saute onion until translucent. Add garlic and saute 1 to 2 minutes

2. Turn off the Sauté function and add all of soup ingredients. Put the lid on and make sure the vent is closed. Press the Manual button and set to cook for approximately 10 minutes. Once the cooking time is over, allow it to release the pressure naturally. Stir in yeast, salt and pepper. Serve.

Taco Soup

[Servings: 12]

Ingredients:

- 15 ½ ounces of Canned Whole Kernel Corn
- 15 ½ ounces of Canned Diced Tomatoes
- 1 ounce of Ranch Dressing Mix
- 10 ounces of Diced Tomatoes with Green Chiles
- 45 ounces of Canned Pinto Beans
- 3 cups of Cooked Ground Beef
- 1 ¼ cups of Diced Onion
- 2 tbsp. Taco Seasoning
- 1 tsp. Salt
- ½ tsp. Black Pepper

Directions:

1. Place all of ingredients into Instant Pot. Lock the cover into place and seal the steam nozzle. Choose the Soup setting and adjust to 10 minutes or set manually for approximately 10 minutes
2. Let the pressure release naturally for 5 minutes, then Quick release any of the remaining pressure. Serve.

Chicken Noodle Soup

[Servings: 8]

Ingredients:

- 2 Boneless Skinless Chicken Breasts
- 8 ounces of Wide Egg Noodles
- 6 Chopped White Button Mushrooms
- 1 Bay Leaf
- 2 Chopped Medium Carrots
- 1 Chopped Celery Stalk
- 1 Small Onion [Roughly Diced]
- 4 cloves of Garlic [Roughly Minced]
- 6 cups of Chicken Stock
- 1 tbsp. Olive Oil
- Kosher Salt
- Ground Black Pepper

Garnish:

- ¼ cup Italian Parsley [Finely Chopped]
- 1 tbsp. Freshly Squeezed Lemon Juice

Directions:

1. Press Sauté button on your Instant Pot and click adjust button to Sauté More function. Wait until indicator on the Instant Pot says Hot. Sauté the mushrooms, onions and garlic. Pour olive oil into pressure cooker. Add in chopped white mushrooms, kosher salt and ground black pepper. Stir to evenly coat mushrooms with olive oil.
2. Mushrooms will start releasing their moisture. Allow the moisture to evaporate and stir occasionally until mushrooms are slightly crisp and browned
3. Add in diced onions, minced garlic and cook until onions softened and fragrant. Should take about 1 to 2 minutes. Add bay leaf, chopped carrots and celery. Stir and season with kosher salt and ground black pepper if you like.
4. Pour ⅓ cup unsalted chicken stock. Scrub all the flavorful brown bits off the bottom of skillet with a wooden spoon. Pour in ⅔ cup chicken stock
5. Partially submerge chicken breasts or drumsticks into the Instant Pot's liquid. Close the lid. Cook at High pressure for 8 minutes + 10 minutes of Natural Release.
6. While chicken is cooking, bring 5 cups of unsalted chicken stock to a boil on stove over a medium-high heat.
7. Shred chicken. Open your Instant Pot lid, remove the bay leaf and chicken. Use a fork to shred chicken.

8. Make chicken soup. Pour 5 cups of unsalted chicken stock into Instant Pot, press the Sauté button and click adjust button to Sauté More function
9. Pour in wide egg noodles and cook until reaching the desired texture. Approximately 4 to 8 minutes. Season chicken soup with kosher salt and ground black pepper. Brighten with freshly squeezed lemon juice. Turn off the heat, add shredded chicken into Instant Pot. Garnish with Italian parsley. Serve.

Sweet Potato Soup

[Servings: 8]

Ingredients:

- 3 cups of Cooked Ground Beef
- 20 ounces of Diced Tomatoes with Green Chiles
- ¼ cup Lime [Juiced]
- 3 tsp. Minced Garlic Cloves
- 1 cup Diced Onion
- 1 cup Cooked Dried Black Beans
- 1 cup Cooked Dried Pinto Beans
- ⅔ cup Diced Sweet Potato
- 1 cup Water
- 2 tbsp. Tomato Paste
- 1 tbsp. Chili Powder
- 1 tbsp. Cumin
- 4 tbsp. Chopped Fresh Cilantro
- ¼ tsp. Dried Oregano
- 1/8 tsp. Salt
- 1/8 tsp. Black Pepper

Directions:

1. Add all of ingredients to Instant Pot, except lime juice and cilantro.
2. Lock the cover into place and seal the steam nozzle. Cook on the Bean / Chili setting or manual for approximately 30 minutes. Naturally release the pressure. Top with cilantro and lime juice. Serve

Macaroni Soup

[Servings: 4]

Ingredients:

- 1 ½ lbs. of Hamburger
- 10 ounces of Elbow Macaroni
- 6 cups of Beef Broth
- 8-ounce can of Tomato Sauce
- 3 stalks of Chopped Celery
- 1 Small Chopped Onion
- ½ tsp. Salt
- ¼ tsp. Pepper
- Shredded or Grated Parmesan Cheese [Optional]

Directions:

1. Sauté hamburger until no longer pink, drain off most of fat. Add celery and onion and saute for 1 to 2 minutes. Press cancel button
2. Add broth and macaroni. Press the Soup button and set for approximately 5 minutes. Do a valve quick release and then stir in 8-ounce can of tomato sauce. Top with some shredded or grated Parmesan cheese. Serve.

Beef Stew with Turnips and Carrots

[Servings: 4]

Ingredients:

- 1 lb. of Beef Stew Meat [Cut into 1-Inch Pieces]
- 1 lb. of Carrots [Cut into 1-Inch Pieces]
- 1 lb. of Turnips [Cut into 1-Inch Pieces]
- 1 cup Dry Red Wine
- 1 cup Bone Broth
- ¼ cup Chopped Fresh Parsley
- ¼ cup Coconut Aminos
- 1 Chopped Medium Red Onion
- 2 tbsp. Coconut Oil
- 2 tbsp. Cassava Flour
- 1 tsp. Dried Thyme
- Salt

Directions:

1. Season beef with salt. Plug in your Instant Pot and press the "Sauté" button. When hot, put 1 tbsp. coconut oil in to melt. Add beef and brown on all sides. Should take approximately 8 minutes total. Remove beef and set to the side.
2. Add remaining fat and onions to your Instant Pot and cook, stirring constantly, until soft. Should take about 5 minutes.
3. Stir in cassava flour and thyme and cook for approximately one minute. Whisk in wine, scraping up any browned bits on the bottom of pot.
4. Stir in broth, carrots, turnips, coconut aminos and reserved beef. Place lid on your Instant Pot and lock into place. Press the "Meat / Stew" button
4. When cooking is complete, allow pressure to release naturally for approximately 10 minutes, then Quick release any of the remaining pressure. Ladle into individual bowls and garnish with parsley. Serve.

Pork Shank Carrots Soup

[Servings: 3]

Ingredients:

- 1 ½ lbs. of Pork Shank
- 1 piece of Thinly Sliced Ginger
- 1 piece of Chenpi
- 2 Large Carrots [Roughly Chopped]
- 1 Large Green Radish [Roughly Chopped]
- 2 Dried Jujubes
- 4 quarts of Cold Running Tap Water
- Sea Salt

Directions:

1. Bring 2 quarts of water to a boil. Then, boil pork shank for 3 minutes to clean and remove any excess fat. Remove pork shank and rinse it in cold tap water. Soak 1 small piece of chenpi in cold water for approximately 20 minutes. Wash dried jujubes with cold running tap water
2. Place all of ingredients into Instant Pot. Pour 2 quarts of cold running tap water into Instant Pot. Do not add any salt. Close the lid and cook at High pressure for 30 minutes. Turn off the heat and Natural release for 20 to 25 minutes. Carefully open the lid and heat up your Instant Pot to bring soup back to a full boil. Add sea salt. Serve.

Healthy Chili

[Servings: 6]

Ingredients:

- 20 fluid ounces of Kettle and Fire's Beef Bone Broth
- 15 ounces of Canned Sliced Beets
- 1 ½ cups of Cooked Ground Beef
- 16 ounces of Canned Pumpkin
- 2 cups of Peeled and Diced Sweet Potato
- 2 cups of Diced Carrot
- 2 tbsp. Apple Cider Vinegar
- 1 ½ tsp. Dried Rosemary
- 1 tsp. Cinnamon
- 3 tsp. Dried Basil
- 1 ½ tsp. Sea Salt

Directions:

1. Place beets into food processor and process until smoothAdd pureed beets and all of the other ingredients into Instant Pot. Lock the cover into place and seal the steam nozzle
2. Choose the Soup setting and adjust to 10 minutes or set manually for approximately 10 minutes. Release the pressure naturally. Serve.

Tuscan Chicken Stew

[Servings: 6]

Ingredients:

- 3 cups of Cooked and Shredded Chicken Boneless Breasts
- 15 ounces of Canned Diced Tomatoes
- 15 ounces of Rinsed and Drained Garbanzo Beans [Canned]
- 1 cup Diced Celery
- 4 cups of Chicken Broth / Stock
- 1 cup Peeled and Diced Red Potato
- 1 cup Diced Leek
- ½ cup Diced Onion
- 1 cup Diced Carrot
- 2 tbsp. Olive Oil
- 1 tsp. Dried Thyme
- ½ tsp. Red Pepper Flakes
- 4 tsp. Minced Garlic Cloves
- ½ tsp. Paprika
- ¼ tsp. Dried Oregano
- ¼ tsp. Dried Basil
- 1 cup Chopped Kale

Directions:

1. Heat olive oil on the Sauté setting in Instant Pot. Add onions, leeks and garlic. Cook until onions are translucent
2. Add in celery and carrots and cook for 2 minutes. Add chicken stock, chicken, potatoes, thyme, garbanzo beans, red pepper flakes, paprika, oregano, basil, kale and diced tomatoes
3. Cover and lock lid. Choose the Soup setting and adjust to 10 minutes or set manually for approximately 10 minutes. Release the pressure naturally. Serve

Potato Soup

[Servings: 4]

Ingredients:

- 5 cups of Diced Yukon Gold Potato
- 16 ounces of Cream Cheese
- 8 cups of Chicken Broth / Stock
- ¼ cup Shredded Cheddar Cheese
- ¼ cup Bacon
- 1 ¼ cups of Diced Onion
- 1 tbsp. Season Salt
- 10 tsp. Minced Garlic Cloves

Directions:

1. Add potatoes, onion, garlic, seasoning and chicken stock to Instant Pot. Lock cover into place and seal the steam nozzle. Choose the Soup setting and adjust to 10 minutes or set manually for approximately 10 minutes.
2. Quick release the pressure. Hit cancel and then sauté. Stir in cream cheese, stirring occasionally for 2 minutes until soup is well blended. Stir well and top with shredded cheese and bacon. Serve.

Bean Soup with Pork

[Servings: 12]

Ingredients:

- 1 ¼ lbs. of Boneless Pork Chops
- 14 ½ ounces of Canned Diced Tomatoes
- 20 ounces of 15 Bean Soup Mix
- ¼ cup Fresh Parsley
- 2 ½ cups of Diced Carrot
- 3 cups of Diced Celery
- 1 cup Diced Onion
- 4 cups of Chicken Broth / Stock
- ⅓ cup Cooked and Diced Bacon
- 3 whole Bay Leaf
- 2 tbsp. Bacon Fat
- 2 tbsp. Dijon Mustard
- 2 tbsp. Worcestershire Sauce
- 1 tbsp. Chili Powder
- 3 tbsp. Lemon Juice
- 4 tsp. Minced Garlic Cloves
- 1 tsp. Black Pepper
- 1 tsp. Sea Salt

Directions:

1. Drain and rinse soaked beans. Set to the side. Heat half of reserved bacon drippings in your Instant Pot using the Sauté function
2. Sear pork chops on both sides until browned. Set to the side. In the remaining bacon drippings, saute onion, celery, carrots and garlic until the onions are translucent.
3. Add diced tomatoes and stir well to combine. In Instant Pot, combine soaked beans, onion/tomato mixture, bacon, pork chops, Worcestershire sauce, bay leaves, mustard, chili powder, pepper, salt and lemon juice.
4. Pour chicken broth over the ingredients and stir gently to combine. Lock the lid into place and seal the steam nozzle
5. Cook on Manual for approximately 18 minutes. Let the pressure release naturally for 5 minutes then release any of the remaining pressure. Remove the bay leaves and pork chops from soup. Cut the meat off bones and return to soup. Stir in fresh parsley. Serve.

Pork Rib and Lotus Root Soup

[Servings: 6]

Ingredients:

- 1 lb. of Pork Side Rib
- 8 ounces of Fresh Lotus Root [Peeled and Sliced into 1/8-Inch Rounds]
- 1 small piece of Ginger [Cut into 3 Slices]
- 6 cups of Water
- 2 tsp. Salt

Directions:

1. Put all of ingredients into Instant Pot. Press the Soup button. Should take about 40 minutes for soup to properly cook. Once finished remove from Instant Pot. Serve

Winter Minestrone

[Servings: 6]

Ingredients:

- 6 cups of Vegetable Broth / Stock
- 1 ½ cups of Diced Carrot
- 1 ¼ cups of Wild Rice
- 1 ½ cups of Canned Cannellini White Beans
- 1 cup Diced Leek
- 1 ¼ cups of Diced Onion
- 1 cup Diced Celery
- 16 ounces of Canned Diced Tomatoes
- 1 tbsp. Olive Oil
- 2 tsp. Dried Oregano
- 1 tsp. Salt
- 4 tsp. Minced Garlic Cloves
- 1 ½ tsp. Black Pepper

Directions:

1. Place all of ingredients in Instant Pot. Lock the lid into place and seal the steam nozzle. Cook on Manual for approximately 10 minutes. Release the pressure naturally. Serve

Rice and Chicken Ranch Soup

[Servings: 8]

Ingredients:

- 2 ½ cups of Cooked and Diced Chicken Boneless Breasts
- 1 ¼ cups of Diced Onion
- 1 ½ cups of Diced Celery
- 1 ½ cups of Diced Carrot
- 1 cup Cooked White Rice [Long-Grain]
- 8 cups of Chicken Broth / Stock
- 3 tsp. Minced Garlic Cloves
- 1 tbsp. Ranch Dressing Mix [Dairy-Free]
- 2 tbsp. Olive Oil
- 2 tbsp. Dijon Mustard
- ½ tsp. Sea Salt
- ¼ tsp. Black Pepper

Directions:

1. Set your Instant Pot to Sauté and heat olive oil. Add onions, carrots and celery and cook for approximately 2 minutes, or until softened. Add garlic and cook for 1 minute. Add chicken, rice, ranch, chicken broth, pepper, salt and mustard. Lock the cover into place and seal the steam nozzle.
2. Choose the Soup setting and adjust to 10 minutes or set manually for approximately 10 minutes. Allow the pressure to release naturally for 5 minutes then release any of the remaining pressure. Serve.

Seared Marinated Artichokes

[Servings: 6]

Ingredients:

- 4 Large Artichokes
- 2 cloves of Minced Garlic
- ¼ cup Olive Oil
- 2 tbsp. Fresh Lemon Juice
- 2 tsp. Balsamic Vinegar
- 1 tsp. Dried Oregano
- ½ tsp. Sea Salt
- ¼ tsp. Fresh Ground Black Pepper

Directions:

1. Wash artichokes under cold water. Using a heavy stainless steel knife cut off stems about 1/2-inch from the base. Pull off lower petals that are small and tough. Cut off the top inch of artichoke. Trim the thorny tips of the petals with kitchen shears.
2. Place artichokes, bottom up, in the inner pot of your Instant Pot fitted with a steamer basket and 2 cups of water. Choose the "Steam" setting and reduce cooking time to approximately 8 minutes.
3. While the artichokes are steaming prepare marinade by placing the lemon juice, olive oil, balsamic vinegar, garlic, oregano, salt and pepper in a small jar with a lid. Shake well to incorporate all of ingredients. Set to the side
4. When the "Steam" cycle is complete, release the pressure and carefully remove artichokes.
5. Allow to cool slightly so you can handle them. Cut artichokes in half. Remove the center cone of purple prickly leaves. This is the choke that protects the heart. Now, scrape away the thistle fuzz covering the artichoke heart. The heart is the meatiest part of the artichoke
6. Drizzle the marinade over warm artichokes. Turning to make sure to coat them well with marinade. Allow them to sit for 30 minutes to overnight. When ready to serve, sear artichokes cut side down on a grill pan or BBQ for 3 to 5 minutes. Serve.

Mango Dal

[Servings: 6]

Ingredients:

- 1 Medium Minced Onion
- 4 cloves of Minced Garlic
- ½ cup Chopped Fresh Cilantro
- 1 cup Chana Dal
- 4 cups of Chicken Broth
- 2 Mango's [Peeled and Diced]
- 1 tbsp. Minced Fresh Ginger
- 1 tbsp. Coconut Oil
- 1 tsp. Ground Cumin
- 1 tsp. Ground Coriander
- 1 tsp. Ground Turmeric
- 1/8 tsp. Cayenne Pepper
- 1 tsp. Sea Salt
- Juice of ½ A Lime

Directions:

1. Place chana dal in colander and rinse until water runs clear. Set your Instant Pot to Sauté to heat it up. Heat coconut oil until melted. Add cumin and sauté until fragrant, about 30 seconds.
2. Add onion; sauté until soft and starting to brown. Should take about 5 minutes. Add garlic, ginger, coriander, cayenne and sea salt and sauté for 1 minute more. Add chana dal, chicken broth and turmeric to Instant Pot. Keep on the Sauté feature and bring to a boil; boil for about 10 minutes removing any foam that comes to the top
3. Add mango's. Place lid on the Instant Pot and lock into place. Press the Beans / Chili button; adjust the time so that the cook time is 20 minutes. When done and pressure has naturally released, remove lid; stir in lime juice and cilantro. You can add rice or chicken to this meal if you desire. Serve.

Spicy Chicken Soup

[Servings: 6 - 8]

Ingredients:

- 4 Boneless Skinless Chicken Breasts
- 2 (14.5-ounce) cans of Peeled and Diced Tomatoes
- 2 (16-ounce) cans of Drained Black Beans
- 15-ounce bag of Frozen Corn
- 2 (14.5-ounce) cans of Chicken Broth
- 1 Large Diced Onion
- 16-ounce jar of Mild Chunky Salsa
- 3 cloves of Minced Garlic
- 2 tbsp. Dried Parsley
- 2 tbsp. Olive Oil
- 1 tbsp. Chili Powder
- 1 tbsp. Onion Powder
- 1 tsp. Garlic Powder
- ½ tsp. Salt
- 1 tsp. Ground Black Pepper
- Shredded Cheese [Optional]
- Tortilla Chips [Optional]
- Sour Cream [Optional]

Directions:

1. Select Sauté and add olive oil to Instant Pot. When oil is hot, add onion and cook, stirring occasionally until onion is tender. Should take about 5 minutes. Add garlic and cook for an additional minute
2. Add remaining ingredients, except beans and corn. Lock the lid in place, select High pressure and cook for 8 minutes. It will take about 20 minutes to come to pressure because there is so much liquid. When the timer beeps, turn off Instant Pot, wait 10 minutes, then do a Quick pressure release
3. Remove chicken breasts from the soup and dice or shred it. Return chicken to soup and stir in black beans and corn. If necessary, select Simmer and bring to a boil, stirring occasionally until beans and corn are heated. Top with shredded cheese, sour cream and tortilla chips, if so desired. Serve

Pho Ga

[Servings: 6]

Ingredients:

- 8 Chicken Drumsticks
- ¼ cup Fish Sauce
- 1 small bunch of Cilantro
- 1 small hand of Ginger [Roughly Sliced]
- 2 Medium Yellow Onions [Split In Half]
- 1 Cinnamon Stick
- 3 Star Anise Pods
- 4 Cloves
- 2 tbsp. Vegetable Oil
- 2 tbsp. Raw Sugar
- 1 tsp. Fennel Seeds
- 1 tsp. Coriander Seeds

To Serve:

- 4 servings of Pho Noodles [Cooked]
- ½ cup Thinly Sliced Scallions
- 1 Small White or Yellow Onion [Thinly Sliced]
- 2 cups of Trimmed Bean Sprouts
- 2 cups of Mixed Herbs [Cilantro; Mint; and Basil]
- 2 Limes [Each Cut into 4 Wedges]
- Thinly sliced Thai Chiles
- Hoisin Sauce
- Sriracha

Directions:

1. Heat oil in your Instant Pot over a high heat. Add halved onions and ginger, cut side down. Cook without moving, reducing the heat if smoking excessively, until onion and ginger are well charred. Should take about 5 minutes. Add cilantro, star anise, cloves, cinnamon, fennel seed, coriander and chicken to pot. Add 2 quarts of water, fish sauce and sugar to the pot.
2. Seal the Instant Pot and bring it to High pressure over high heat. Cook on high pressure for approximately 20 minutes, then shock release pressure valve naturally.

3. Open your Instant Pot and transfer chicken legs to plate. Pour broth through a fine mesh strainer into a clean pot and discard the solids
4. Skim any scum off the surface of broth using a ladle, but leave the small bubbles of fat intact. Season broth to taste with more fish sauce and sugar if so desired
5. Place re-hydrated Pho noodles in individual noodle bowls. Top with chicken legs, sliced onions and scallions. Pour hot broth over chicken and noodles. Put out remaining ingredients so everyone can make their dish to their own personal preference. Serve.

Sweet Carrot Puree

[Servings: 4]

Ingredients:

- 1 ½ lbs. of Carrots [Roughly Chopped]
- 1 cup Water
- 1 tbsp. Butter [Room Temperature]
- 1 tbsp. Honey
- ¼ tsp. Sea Salt
- Brown Sugar [Optional]

Directions:

1. Clean, peel and dry carrots. Roughly chop them into small-sized pieces. Pour 1 cup water in Instant Pot. Place chopped carrots into your Instant Pot in a steamer basket. Close the lid and cook at High pressure for 4 minutes, then Quick release. Remove carrots and dry
2. Place carrots in a deep bowl. Use an immersion hand blender to blend carrots until desired consistency. Add butter, honey and sea salt to carrot puree. Mix together well. Taste carrot puree and add brown sugar if you desire. Serve.

Potato Risotto

[Servings: 6]

Ingredients:

- 1 Chopped Medium Yellow Onion
- 1 Medium Golden or Red Potato [Chopped into 1/2-Inch Cubes]
- ¼ cup White Wine
- 4 cups of Salt-Free Vegetable Stock
- 2 cups of Arborio
- 1 tbsp. Olive Oil
- 1 tbsp. Tomato Paste
- 1 ½ tsp. Salt
- Sprigs of Thyme

Directions:

1. Set your Instant Pot to Sauté mode. Add olive oil and onion and sauté, stirring frequently until onion begins to soften. Add rice and stir constantly until it absorbs the onion juice and begins to dry again. Should take about 5 minutes
2. Add wine and stir constantly until rice absorbs all of the wine. Add potatoes, stock, tomato paste and salt. Close lid and cook for approximately 5 minutes at High pressure. When time is up, open your Instant Pot with Natural pressure release [twist the valve on the lid to the "open" or "venting" position]. Remove lid and tilt it away from you
3. Mix the contents and remove the inner pot from your Instant Pot onto a heat-safe surface [to keep risotto from overcooking]. Sprinkle with fresh thyme. Serve

Smoky Ham Hock and Pinto Bean Soup

[Servings: 3]

Ingredients:

- 2 lbs. of Smoked Ham Hock
- 5 cups of Unsalted Chicken Stock
- 2 cups of Pinto Beans
- 6 cloves of Crushed Garlic
- 1 Sliced Small Onion
- 1 tsp. Cumin Powder
- 2 Bay Leaves
- Pinch of Dried Oregano
- Pinch of Ground Black Pepper
- Kosher Salt
- Cilantro [For Garnish]
- Minced Tomatoes [For Garnish]

Directions:

1. Clean pinto beans with cold running tap water. Place all of ingredients [smoked ham hock, onion, garlic cloves, cumin powder, dried oregano, ground black pepper, bay leaves, pinto beans and unsalted chicken stock] into Instant Pot
2. Lock your Instant Pot lid in place and cook at High pressure for 50 minutes. Turn off the heat and do a full Natural release. Should take roughly 20 minutes. Season with kosher salt. Garnish with cilantro and minced tomatoes. Serve.

Cheesy Potato Soup

[Servings: 6]

Ingredients:

- 32 ounces of O'Brien Hashed Brown Potatoes [Frozen]
- ½ cup Diced Onion
- 3 cups of Milk
- 3 cups of Shredded Mild Cheddar Cheese
- 3 cups of Chicken Broth / Stock
- ⅔ cup Diced Celery
- 1 ½ tsp. Salt
- ¾ tsp. Black Pepper

Directions:

1. Place chicken broth, hash browns, salt, pepper, celery and onions into Instant Pot. Lock cover into place and seal the steam nozzle. Select the Soup setting and adjust to 10 minutes or set manually for approximately 10 minutes. Quick release the pressure
2. Change the setting to Sauté and add milk and cheese. Stir until cheese is melted and soup is thoroughly warmed. Serve.

Orange Brussels Sprouts

[Servings: 8]

Ingredients:

- 2 lbs. of Brussels Sprouts [Trimmed]
- ¼ cup Freshly Squeezed Orange Juice
- 1 tbsp. Earth Balance Buttery Spread
- 2 tbsp. Maple Syrup
- 1 tsp. Grated Orange Zest
- ¼ tsp. Black Pepper
- ½ tsp. Salt

Directions:

1. Place all of ingredients in Instant Pot. Cover with lid. Make sure that the Quick release switch is closed. Push the Manual button and set it for approximately 3 to 4 minutes. When the time is up, hit the off button and quick release the pressure. Stir until Brussels sprouts are evenly covered sauce. Serve.

Baked Potatoes

[Servings: 4]

Ingredients:

- 3 lbs. of Potatoes [Peeled and Chopped]

Directions:

1. Insert steamer rack into Instant Pot. Add about 1 cup water into Instant Pot. Add potatoes. Close the lid and turn the sealing vent to "sealed". Click the Manual button and reduce the time to approximately 10 minutes
2. Once cooking is finished let the pressure valve release naturally. Should take about 20 minutes. Open the lid and remove potatoes
3. Potatoes come out nice and soft. If you want them crispier place them on baking sheet in oven for approximately 10 minutes at 350 degrees. Serve.

Corn On the Cob

[Servings: 4]

Ingredients:

- 4 ears of Corn On the Cob
- 2 tbsp. Shacha Sauce
- 1 tbsp. Sugar
- 3 tbsp. Light Soy Sauce
- 1 tsp. Garlic Powder
- ¼ tsp. Sesame Oil

Directions:

1. Pour 1 cup cold running tap water into Instant Pot. Place trivet into your Instant Pot and place 4 ears of corn on the cob onto trivet. Close lid and cook at High pressure for approximately 1 to 2 minutes. Turn off the heat and Quick release. Open lid carefully.
2. While the corn on the cob is cooking in Instant Pot, preheat oven to 450 degrees. Mix light soy sauce, Shacha sauce, sugar, garlic powder and sesame oil in a small-sized mixing bowl.
3. Brush the sauce all over corn on the cob on all sides with basting brush. Place them on a rack with baking tray in the oven for approximately 5 to 10 minutes. Serve.

Black Eyed Pea Soup

[Servings: 4]

Ingredients:

- 10 ounces of Frozen Sliced Okra [Defrosted]
- 1 clove of Minced Garlic [Large]
- 1 Large Onion [Coarsely Chopped]
- 2 cups of Dried Black-Eyed Peas [Picked Over and Rinsed]
- 3 Large Carrots [Peeled and Sliced]
- 2 tbsp. Olive Oil
- 6 cups of Chicken Broth
- Salt
- 1 Smoked Ham Hock [Optional]
- Tabasco [Optional]

Directions:

1. Select Sauté and add oil to Instant Pot. When oil is hot, add onion and cook, stirring occasionally until onion is tender. Should take about 5 minutes. Add garlic and cook for an additional minute
2. Add peas, broth and ham hock [if using]. Lock the lid in place, select High pressure and cook for 10 minutes. When the timer beeps, turn off your Instant Pot and do a Quick pressure release. When the valve drops carefully remove lid

3. Remove ham hock and add carrots and okra. Cut off the meat and stir it into soup along with the tabasco [if using] and salt to taste. Simmer until carrots and okra are cooked. Should take approximately 3 to 4 minutes. Adjust the seasonings if necessary. Serve.

Savory Spaghetti Sauce with Bacon

[Servings: 8]

Ingredients:

- 3 cups of Cooked Ground Beef
- 12 ounces of Tomato Paste
- 1 ½ cups of Diced Bacon
- 64 fluid ounces of Tomato Juice
- 2 ½ cups of Diced Onion
- 4 tbsp. Dried Parsley
- 1 tsp. Cinnamon
- 3 tsp. Worcestershire Sauce
- 1 tsp. Paprika
- 4 tsp. Celery Seed
- ¼ tsp. Garlic Powder
- ½ tsp. Ground Cloves
- 4 tsp. Sugar
- 4 tsp. Salt
- ½ tsp. Black Pepper

Directions:

1. Place bacon in your Instant Pot and saute until fully cooked. Remove from pot but leave the drippings. Sauté onion for 2 minutes
2. Add cooked bacon and the remaining ingredients into Instant Pot. Lock the lid into place and seal the steam nozzle. Cook on the Meat setting or manually for approximately 15 minutes. Quick release the pressure. Add over spaghetti. Serve.

Awesome Mexican Green Rice

[Servings: 3]

Ingredients:

- 1 ¼ cups of Low-Sodium Chicken or Vegetable Broth
- 1/2 cup Fresh Cilantro
- 1 cup Uncooked Long-Grain Rice
- 1/4 cup Green Salsa
- Flesh of 1/2 Large Ripe Avocado
- Freshly Ground Pepper
- Salt

Directions:

1. Add broth and rice to Instant Pot. Stir and lock lid in place. Select High pressure and 3 minutes cook time. When the timer beeps, turn the Instant Pot off and use a Natural pressure release for 10 minutes. After 10 minutes do a Quick pressure release
2. Fluff the rice with a fork and let cool to warm. Blend in a blender avocado, cilantro and salsa, adding a little water as needed to blend smoothly to the consistency of sour cream. Stir into rice. Season with salt and pepper. Serve.

Maple Bacon Acorn Squash

[**Servings:** 6]

Ingredients:

- 4 lbs. of Acorn Squash
- ½ cup Cooked and Diced Bacon
- 2 tbsp. Butter
- 2 tbsp. Maple Syrup
- 1 tsp. Sea Salt

Directions:

1. Wash the outside of acorn squash. Pour 1 cup water into Instant Pot and place trivet inside. Set squash on the trivet. Lock lid into place and seal the steam nozzle. Select the manual option and set for approximately 8 minutes. Quick release the pressure. Let it cool slightly.
2. Using oven mitts, carefully remove squash. Cut in half and remove any seeds. The squash will not be fully cooked. Place squash back into Instant Pot. Lock lid into place and seal the steam nozzle.
3. Select the Manual option and set for approximately 8 more minutes. Quick release the pressure. Let it cool slightly. Remove squash and scrape the flesh from the shell. Mash squash and add the butter and maple syrup. Gently fold in bacon and sea salt. Serve.

Zuppa Toscana

[**Servings:** 8]

Ingredients:

- 1 lb. of Ground Chicken Sausage
- 3 [14.5]-ounce cans of Chicken Broth [Divided]
- 6 slices of Diced Bacon
- 12-ounce can of Evaporated Milk
- 2 cups of Fresh Spinach [Roughly Chopped]
- 1 cup Parmesan Cheese [Shredded and Divided]
- 3 Large Russet Potatoes [Cubed]
- 1 cup Diced Onion
- 3 cloves of Minced Garlic
- 3 tbsp. Corn Starch
- 1 tbsp. Butter
- 1/8 tsp. Red Pepper Flakes
- ½ tsp. Salt
- ½ tsp. Black Pepper

Directions:

1. Select Sauté and add bacon to Instant Pot. Cook until crisp and remove to a plate lined with paper towels. Add sausage to the Instant Pot and cook until browned. Remove to second plate lined with paper towels.
2. Add butter to Instant Pot. When butter is melted, add onion and cook, stirring occasionally until onion is tender. Should take about 5 minutes. Add garlic and cook 1 minute more. Add 1 can of chicken broth, salt, pepper and red pepper flakes to Instant Pot.
3. Put steamer basket in Instant Pot. Add diced potatoes. Lock the lid in place, select High pressure and cook for 4 minutes
4. When the timer beeps, turn off your Instant Pot and do a Quick pressure release. Carefully remove potatoes and steamer basket from Instant Pot. Add remaining 2 cans of chicken broth to Instant Pot.
5. In a mixing bowl, dissolve cornstarch in a small amount of evaporated milk. Add to your Instant Pot along with the remainder of evaporated milk. Select Simmer and bring to a boil, stirring often
6. When soup thickens, stir in ¾ cup Parmesan cheese, spinach, browned sausage, potatoes and half of crispy bacon. Top with remaining Parmesan cheese and bacon. Serve.

Corn Chowder

[**Servings:** 7]

Ingredients:

- 6 ears of Fresh Corn
- 1/2 cup Chopped Onion
- 4 slices of Cooked and Diced Bacon
- 2 Medium Diced Potatoes
- 3 cups of Milk
- 3 cups of Water
- 2 tbsp. Water
- 4 tbsp. Butter
- 2 tbsp. Fresh Parsley
- 2 tbsp. Cornstarch
- 1/8 tsp. Ground Red Pepper
- Salt
- Freshly Ground Black Pepper

Directions:

1. Shuck corn. Use sharp knife to cut off the kernels. Select Sauté and add butter to Instant Pot. When butter is melted, add onion and cook, stirring occasionally until onion is tender. Should take about 3 minutes
2. Add 3 cups of water and corncobs to Instant Pot. Lock the lid in place, select High pressure and cook for 10 minutes. When the timer beeps, turn off your Instant Pot and do a Quick pressure release.
3. Carefully remove corncobs and discard them. Leave corncob broth in the Instant Pot. Put steamer basket in Instant Pot. Add diced potatoes and corn kernels. Lock the lid in place, select High pressure and cook for 4 minutes
4. When the timer beeps, turn off your Instant Pot and do a Quick pressure release. Carefully remove steamer basket, corn and potatoes from Instant Pot.
5. In a small-sized bowl, dissolve cornstarch in 2 tbsp. water. Select Simmer and add cornstarch mixture to your Instant Pot stirring constantly until soup thickens. Stir in milk, cayenne pepper, diced potatoes, corn kernels, bacon and parsley. Add salt and pepper to taste. Heat through but do not bring to a boil. Serve.

Taco Chicken Soup

[**Servings:** 6]

Ingredients:

- 3 ¾ cups of Diced Chicken Boneless Breasts
- 20 ounces of Drained Diced Tomatoes with Green Chiles
- 15 ounces of Drained and Rinsed Black Beans [Canned]
- 8 ounces of Tomato Sauce
- 16 ounces of Chili Beans
- 1 ¼ ounces of Taco Seasoning
- 1 cup Diced Onion

Directions:

1. Place all ingredients into Instant Pot. Lock the cover into place and seal the steam nozzle. Choose Soup setting and adjust to 10 minutes or set manually for approximately 10 minutes
2. Let the pressure release naturally for 5 minutes, then release any of the remaining pressure. Serve.

Pumpkin Chicken Corn Chowder

[**Servings:** 5]

Ingredients:

- 2 Large Boneless Skinless Chicken Breasts [Uncooked and Diced]
- 2 Large Russet Potatoes [Cubed]
- 15-ounce can of Pumpkin Puree
- 2 (14.5-ounce) cans of Chicken Broth
- 1 cup Diced Onion
- 2 cup Frozen Corn
- ½ cup Half and Half
- 1 clove of Minced Garlic
- 2 tbsp. Butter
- ½ tsp. Italian Seasoning
- 1/8 tsp. Freshly Grated Nutmeg
- 1/8 tsp. Dried Red Pepper Flakes
- ¼ tsp. Freshly Ground Black Pepper
- Salt
- Crumbled Bacon [Optional]
- Fresh Parsley [Optional]

Directions:

1. Add butter to Instant Pot. When butter is melted, add onion and cook, stirring occasionally until onion is tender. Should take about 5 minutes. Add garlic and cook for 1 minute more. Add chicken broth, pumpkin puree, pepper, Italian seasoning, red pepper flakes and nutmeg to Instant Pot. Stir well to combine
2. Add diced potatoes and diced chicken. Lock the lid in place, select High pressure and cook for 4 minutes. When the timer beeps, turn off your Instant Pot and do a Quick pressure release. Stir in corn and half and half. Add salt and pepper to taste. Top with crumbled bacon and chopped parsley. Serve.

Garlic Mushrooms with White Beans and Farro

[**Servings:** 4]

Ingredients:

- 1 cup Dried White Navy Beans
- ½ Finely Chopped Jalapeno Pepper
- 2 Medium Tomatoes [Diced]
- 9 cloves of Garlic [Finely Chopped]
- ½ cup Farro
- 3 cups of Mushrooms [Finely Chopped]
- 1 tbsp. Thai Red Curry Paste
- 2 tbsp. Onion Powder
- 2 tbsp. Hulled Barley
- 1 tbsp. Shallot Powder
- Chopped Cilantro
- Chopped Scallions
- Water

Directions:

1. Cook all of ingredients except tomatoes, cilantro and scallions in your Instant Pot on the "Soup" setting. Should take approximately 30 minutes. Stir in diced tomatoes when it has finished cooking and top with cilantro and scallions. Serve.

Dessert Recipes

Steamed Carrot Pudding Cake

[Servings: 8]

Ingredients:

- ½ cup Brown Sugar
- ½ cup Grated Carrots
- ½ cup Chopped Pecans or Walnuts
- ½ cup Raisins
- ½ cup Flour
- 1 cup Dry Bread Crumbs
- ⅔ cup Shortening [Frozen and Grated]
- ¼ cup Molasses
- 2 Large Eggs
- ¼ tsp. Nutmeg
- ¼ tsp. Salt
- ½ tsp. Allspice
- ½ tsp. Baking Soda
- ½ tsp. Cinnamon

Spiced Rum Sauce:

- ¼ cup Heavy Cream
- ½ cup Brown Sugar
- 4 tbsp. Butter
- 2 tbsp. Rum
- ¼ tsp. Ground Cinnamon

Directions:

1. In a large-sized mixing bowl, whisk together brown sugar, eggs and molasses. Add flour and spices and stir until blended. Fold in shortening, raisins, carrots, nuts and bread crumbs. Spoon batter into half sized bundt pan sprayed with a non-stick spray. Cover with foil and poke a hole in the middle of tin foil.
2. Prepare a foil sling for lifting the pan out of your Instant Pot by taking an 18-inch strip of foil and folding it lengthwise twice. Pour 1 ½ cups of water into your Instant Pot and place the trivet in the bottom. Center the bundt pan on the foil strip and lower it into Instant Pot. Fold the foil strips down so that they do not interfere with closing lid.
3. Lock lid in place. Select High pressure and set the timer for 60 minutes. When the beep sounds, turn off your Instant Pot and use a Natural pressure release to release any of the pressure.
4. Carefully remove bundt pan to a wire rack to cool uncovered for 10 minutes. After 10 minutes, place it on a serving platter
5. **Spiced Rum Sauce:** Stir brown sugar and butter in a heavy medium saucepan over a medium heat until melted and smooth. Should take about 2 minutes. Add cream, rum and cinnamon and simmer until sauce thickens slightly. Should take about 5 minutes. Serve.

Black Chocolate Cake

[Servings: 3]

Ingredients:

- 7 ounce Ghirardelli Chocolate 60% Cacao Bittersweet Chocolate Baking Chips
- ¼ cup Flour
- ½ cup Sugar
- 3 Eggs
- 4 tbsp. Butter

Directions:

1. Melt chocolate and butter together. Add sugar, flour and eggs. Beat. Put in ramekin. Place on the trivet in your Instant Pot and add 250ml water in pot.
2. Cook for 12 minutes on the "Manual" setting and then Quick release. Serve

Black Rice Pudding with Dried Cherries

[**Servings:** 3]

Ingredients:

- 1 cup Rinsed Black Rice
- ¾ cup Half and Half
- 1 cup Milk
- 1 ½ cups of Water
- ½ cup Sugar
- ⅔ cup Dried Cherries
- 1 tbsp. Butter
- 1 tbsp. Butter
- 1 tsp. Vanilla Extract
- 2 Eggs
- ¼ tsp. Salt

Directions:

1. In Instant Pot, combine rice, water, salt and butter. Lock lid in place and select High pressure and 22 minutes cook time. When the beep sounds turn off your Instant Pot and use a Natural pressure release for 10 minutes. After 10 minutes, release any of remaining pressure with a Quick pressure release.
2. Add milk and sugar to rice in Instant Pot. Select Sauté and heat until sugar is dissolved, stir occasionally. Whisk eggs with half and half and vanilla
3. Pour through a fine mesh strainer into Instant Pot. Cook, stirring constantly until mixture just starts to boil. Turn off Instant Pot. Stir in cherries. Pour into serving dishes cool then chill. Pudding will thicken as it cools, so you may want to add a little extra half and half if you're serving it cold. Serve.

Raisin Bread Pudding with Caramel Pecan Sauce

[**Servings:** 5]

Ingredients:

- 7 slices of Cubed and Toasted Cinnamon Bread [3/4-Inch Thick]
- ½ cup Raisins
- 3 Eggs [Beaten]
- 3 cups of Whole Milk
- ½ cup Packed Brown Sugar
- 4 tbsp. Melted Butter
- ½ tsp. Ground Cinnamon
- 1 tsp. Vanilla Extract
- ¼ tsp. Salt

Caramel Pecan Sauce:

- ¼ cup Corn Syrup
- ¾ cup Brown Sugar
- ½ cup Toasted and Chopped Pecans
- 2 tbsp. Butter
- 2 tbsp. Heavy Cream
- 1 tsp. Vanilla Extract
- ½ tsp. Salt

Directions:

1. Cube bread and toast on a rimmed cookie sheet in a 350-degree oven for approximately 20 minutes stirring occasionally. Cool bread before continuing with recipe. Can be done earlier in the day or the night before.
2. In large-sized bowl, whisk together melted butter, milk, brown sugar, vanilla, beaten eggs, salt and cinnamon. Mix in cubed bread and raisins. Allow it to rest for 20 minutes until bread absorbs the milk, stirring occasionally
3. Pour bread pudding into a buttered 1 1/2-quart glass or metal baking dish. [Be sure it fits in Instant Pot.] Cover dish with foil. Prepare a foil sling for lifting dish out of your Instant Pot by taking an 18-inch strip of foil and folding it lengthwise twice.
4. Pour 1 ½ cups water into your Instant Pot and place the trivet in the bottom. Center dish on the foil strip and lower it into Instant Pot
5. Lock lid in place. Select High pressure and set the timer for 20 minutes. When the beep sounds, turn off your Instant Pot and do a Quick pressure release to release the pressure. When the valve drops

carefully remove lid. Remove dish from Instant Pot. If desired, put dish in a preheated 350-degree oven for 5 to 10 minutes to crisp up the top
6. In a small-sized saucepan, combine brown sugar, heavy cream, corn syrup, butter and salt. Cook over a medium heat, stirring constantly until sauce comes to a boil. Reduce the heat and simmer until sugar is dissolved and sauce is smooth. Stir in vanilla and chopped pecans. Serve.

Pina Colada Rice Pudding

[Servings: 8]

Ingredients:

- 1 cup Arborio Rice
- ½ cup Milk
- 8-ounce can of Pineapple Tidbits [Well Drained and Cut In Half]
- ½ cup Sugar
- 1 tbsp. Coconut Oil
- 2 Eggs
- 14-ounce can of Coconut Milk
- 1 ½ cups of Water
- ½ tsp. Vanilla Extract
- ¼ tsp. Salt
- Whipped Cream [Optional]
- Maraschino Cherry [Optional]
- Toasted Coconut [Optional]

Directions:

1. In Instant Pot, combine rice, oil, water and salt. Lock lid in place and select High pressure and 3 minutes cook time. When the beep sounds turn off your Instant Pot and use a Natural pressure release for 10 minutes. After 10 minutes, release any of the remaining pressure with a Quick pressure release. Add coconut milk and sugar to rice in Instant Pot. Stir well to combine
2. In a small-sized mixing bowl, whisk eggs with milk and vanilla. Pour through a fine mesh strainer into Instant Pot. Select Sauté and cook, stirring constantly, until mixture just starts to boil. Turn off Instant Pot. Stir in pineapple tidbits
3. Pour into serving dishes and chill. Pudding will thicken as it cools. Top with whipped cream, toasted coconut and a maraschino cherry if desired. Serve.

Orange Swirl Cheesecake

[Servings: 8]

Ingredients:

- 1 cup Crushed Oreo Cookie Crumbs [12 Oreos]
- 2 tbsp. Melted Butter

Filling:

- 16 ounces of Cream Cheese [Room Temperature]
- 2 tbsp. Sour Cream
- 2 Eggs
- ½ cup Melted and Cooled Orange Candy Melts
- ½ cup Sugar
- 1 tsp. Vanilla Extract
- 1 tbsp. Orange Zest

Directions:

1. Prepare a 7-inch springform pan by coating it with a non-stick spray. In a small-sized bowl, combine Oreo cookie crumbs and butter. Spread evenly in the bottom and 1-inch up the side of pan. Place in freezer for 10 minutes. Place 8 ounces of cream cheese into mixing bowl. Add ¼ cup sugar and beat at a medium speed until smooth. Blend in sour cream and vanilla. Mix in one egg until blended. Don't over mix
2. In a second mixing bowl, place 8 ounces of cream cheese and add ¼ cup sugar and beat until smooth. Gradually beat in melted candy melts. Mix in one egg until blended. Stir in orange zest.

3. Scatter dollops of vanilla batter on top of crust alternating with dollops of orange batter. Use a skewer to swirl the orange and vanilla batters together
4. Pour 1 cup water into your Instant Pot and place the trivet in the bottom. Carefully center the filled pan on a foil sling and lower it into Instant Pot. Fold foil sling down so that it doesn't interfere with closing lid.
5. Lock lid in place. Select High pressure and set the timer for approximately 25 minutes. When the beep sounds, turn off your Instant Pot and use a Natural pressure release for 10 minutes and then do a quick pressure release to release any of the remaining pressure
1. When the valve drops carefully remove lid. Remove cheesecake and check the cheesecake to see if the middle is set but slightly jiggly like a set jello. If not, cook the cheesecake an additional 5 minutes. Use the corner of a paper towel to soak up any water on top of cheesecake.
6. Remove the springform pan to a wire rack to cool. When cheesecake is cooled, refrigerate covered with plastic wrap for at least 4 hours. Refrigerate until ready to serve. Decorate with whipped cream, grated orange candy melts and Oreo cookie crumbs. Serve.

Pumpkin Chocolate Chip Bundt Cake

[Servings: 8]

Ingredients:

- 1 ½ cups of All-Purpose Flour
- ½ cup Butter [Softened]
- 1 cup Granulated Sugar
- 1 cup Pumpkin Puree
- ¾ cup Mini Chocolate Chips
- 1 tsp. Ground Cinnamon
- ½ tsp. Pumpkin Pie Spice
- ½ tsp. Baking Soda
- ½ tsp. Baking Powder
- 2 Large Eggs
- ¼ tsp. Salt

Directions:

1. In medium-sized bowl, mix flour, salt, spices, baking soda and baking powder and set to the side. In the bowl of stand mixer cream butter and the sugar until fluffy. Should take about two minutes. Add eggs one at a time mixing well after each addition. Add pumpkin and mix until well combined
2. Add dry ingredients mixing until combined. Stir in chocolate chips. Spoon batter into half sized bundt pan sprayed with a non-stick spray. Cover with foil
3. Pour 1 ½ cups of water into your Instant Pot and place the trivet in the bottom. Put the bundt pan on the trivet. [Use a foil sling to help make removing the bundt pan easier.]
4. Lock lid in place. Select High pressure and set the timer for 25 minutes. When the beep sounds, turn off your Instant Pot and use a Natural pressure release for 10 minutes and then do a Quick pressure release to release any of the remaining pressure. When the valve drops carefully remove lid.
5. Carefully remove the bundt pan to a wire rack to cool uncovered for 10 minutes. After 10 minutes, remove from pan and cool on a wire rack. Serve

Candied Lemon Peels

[Servings: 4]

Ingredients:

- 1 lb. of Organic Lemons
- 5 cups of Water
- 2 ¼ cups of White Granulated Sugar [Divided]

Directions:

1. Wash lemons well, using a scrubby sponge to clean the surface. Slice lemon in half lengthwise and juice. Slice off the nub [where the lemon was attached to the three] at the tip and then slice each half in quarters.
2. Hold the quarters flat on cutting board and peel or slice out the pulp. You can use a melon-baller. Slice the de-pulped lemon quarters into thin strips. Should be about as wide as the lemon peel is thick.
3. To your Instant Pot add lemon peel strips and four cups of water. Cook for 3 minutes at High pressure. When time is up, open cooker by releasing the pressure naturally. Strain the lemon peel strips and rinse them. Then, discard cooking water and rinse out the Instant Pot
4. Add 2 cups of sugar, 1 cup water and lemon strips. Cook for 10 minutes at High pressure
5. When time is up, open Instant pot with the Natural release method - move the cooker off the burner and wait for the pressure to come down on its own. Should take about 10 minutes. Disengage the "keep warm" mode or unplug the cooker and open when the pressure indicator has gone down. Should take 20 to 30 minutes.
6. Strain peels, saving the delicate syrup if you like for another use and spread the peels on a cutting board or parchment paper to cool for approximately 15 minutes or more.
7. Gently toss four to five peels at a time in a small plate of sugar to coat. Shake off the excess and lay them down on a new parchment on a sheet pan that can fit in refrigerator
8. Put sheet pan with the sugared-coated candied lemon peels in refrigerator uncovered for at least 4 hours to dry completely. Serve.

Peanut Butter Cup Cheesecake

[Servings: 10]

Ingredients:

- 1 cup Crushed Oreo Cookie Crumbs
- 2 tbsp. Melted Butter

Filling:

- 12 ounces of Cream Cheese [Room Temperature]
- ½ cup Smooth Peanut Butter
- ¾ cup Semisweet Chocolate Chips
- 2 Eggs [Room Temperature]
- ½ cup Sugar
- ¼ cup Heavy Cream
- 1 ½ tsp. Vanilla Extract
- 1 tbsp. All-Purpose Flour
- 1 Egg Yolk [Room Temperature]

Topping:

- 6 ounces of Finely Chopped Milk Chocolate
- ⅓ cup Heavy Cream
- ⅔ cup Coarsely Chopped Peanut Butter Cups

Directions:

1. Prepare 7-inch springform pan by coating it with non-stick spray. In a small-sized bowl, combine Oreo cookie crumbs and butter. Spread evenly into the bottom and up the side of pan. Place in freezer for 10 minutes

2. In a mixing bowl, mix cream cheese and sugar at a medium speed until smooth, blend in peanut butter, heavy cream, flour and vanilla. Mix in eggs one at a time until blended. Don't over mix. Stir in chocolate chips.
3. Pour batter into springform pan on top of crust. Cover top of the springform pan with aluminum foil. Pour 1 cup water into Instant Pot and place the trivet in the bottom. Carefully center the filled pan on a foil sling and lower it into Instant Pot. Fold the foil sling down so that it doesn't interfere with closing lid.
4. Lock the lid in place. Select High pressure and set the timer for 50 minutes. When the beep sounds, turn off Instant Pot. Use a Natural pressure release for 10 minutes and then do a Quick pressure release to release any of the remaining pressure. When the valve drops carefully remove lid. Remove cheesecake and check the cheesecake to see if the middle is set. If not, cook the cheesecake an additional 5 minutes
5. Remove the springform pan to a wire rack to cool. Remove aluminum foil. When cheesecake is cooled, refrigerate covered with plastic wrap for at least 4 hours
6. When cheesecake is chilled, prepare topping. Place half of chocolate in a mixing bowl. Heat heavy cream on a medium-high heat until it comes to a boil. Remove from heat and immediately pour cream over chocolate and stir until chocolate is completely melted. Add remaining chocolate and stir until chocolate is completely melted. Cool until ganache is thickened but is still thin enough to drip down the sides of cheesecake.
7. Spoon chocolate ganache on top of cheesecake, spreading to edges and letting the ganache drip down the sides. Pile coarsely chopped peanut butter cup chocolates on top. Refrigerate until ready to serve. Serve.

Delicious Pumpkin Pie

[Servings: 8]

Ingredients:

Crust:

- ½ cup Crushed Pecan Sandies [About 6 Cookies]
- ⅓ cup Chopped Toasted Pecans
- 2 tbsp. Melted Butter

Filling:

- ½ cup Light Brown Sugar
- ½ cup Evaporated Milk
- 1 ½ cups of Solid Pack Pumpkin
- 1 ½ tsp. Pumpkin Pie Spice
- 1 Egg [Beaten]
- ½ tsp. Salt
- Whipped Cream [Optional]

Directions:

1. Prepare a 7-inch springform pan by coating it with non-stick spray. In bowl, combine cookie crumbs, chopped pecans and butter. Spread evenly into the bottom and about an inch up the side of pan. Place in freezer for 10 minutes.
2. In a large-sized bowl combine salt, sugar and pumpkin pie spice. Whisk in pumpkin, egg and evaporated milk. Pour into pie crust. Cover top of springform pan with aluminum foil
3. Pour 1 cup water into Instant Pot and place the trivet in the bottom. Carefully center the filled pan on a foil sling and lower it into Instant Pot. Fold the foil sling down so that it doesn't interfere with closing the lid.
4. Lock lid in place. Select High pressure and set the timer for 35 minutes. When the beep sounds, turn off the Instant Pot. Use a Natural pressure release for 10 minutes and then do a Quick pressure release to release any of the remaining pressure.
5. When the valve drops carefully remove lid. Remove pie and check to see if the middle is set. If not, cook an additional 5 minutes. Remove the springform pan to a wire rack to cool. Remove aluminum foil. When pie is cooled, refrigerate covered with plastic wrap for at least 4 hours. Top with whipped cream if you desire. Serve.

Cheesecake with Toffee Pecan Shortbread Cookie Crust

[Servings: 8]

Ingredients:

Crust:

- ½ cup Crushed Shortbread Toffee Cookies [About 6 Cookies]
- ⅓ cup Chopped Pecans
- 2 tbsp. Melted Butter

Filling:

- 2 8-ounce packages of Cream Cheese [Room Temperature]
- 3 Eggs [Room Temperature]
- ⅓ cup Heavy Cream
- ¾ cup Sugar
- ⅓ cup Sour Cream
- 2 tsp. Vanilla Extract
- 2 tbsp. All-Purpose Flour
- Caramel Ice Cream [Optional]
- Grated Chocolate [Optional]
- Toffee Bits [Optional]

Directions:

1. Prepare 7-inch springform pan by greasing it or coating it with non-stick spray. In bowl, combine cookie crumbs, butter and chopped pecans. Spread evenly into the bottom and up the side of pan. Place in freezer for 10 minutes
2. In mixing bowl, mix cream cheese and sugar at a medium speed until smooth, blend in heavy cream, vanilla, sour cream and flour. Mix in eggs one at a time until incorporated. Don't over mix. Pour batter into the prepared crust
3. Place the trivet in the bottom of Instant Pot. Add 1 cup water and lower springform pan with a sling onto the trivet. Lock lid in place, set your Instant Pot to High pressure and the timer to 30 minutes. Allow 10 minutes of Natural release then perform a Quick release
4. Allow it to cool 1 to 2 hours before placing in refrigerator for an additional 2 to 3 hours. If desired, top with caramel ice cream topping, toffee bits, chopped pecans and grated chocolate. Serve.

Mango Coconut Rice Pudding

[Servings: 4]

Ingredients:

- 13.5-ounce can of Light Coconut Milk
- ¾ cup Arborio Rice
- ⅓ cup Brown Sugar
- ½ cup Half and Half
- 1 ½ cups of Water
- 1 Mango [Peeled and Cubed]
- 1 tsp. Vanilla
- 1 tsp. Salt

Garnish:

- ¼ cup Shredded Coconut [Pulsed in Food Processor]
- ¼ cup Almonds [Pulsed in Food Processor]

Directions:

1. Add rice, water, coconut milk, sugar and salt to Instant Pot. Use manual setting and set the time to 7 minutes at High pressure
2. Allow the cooker to cool down naturally. Unlock lid and uncover rice. Add in half and half, vanilla and chopped mango. Stir well together. Place in small-sized bowls with toasted coconut and almonds over the top. Serve.

Key Lime Pie

[Servings: 8]

Ingredients:

Graham Cracker Crust:

- ¾ cup Graham Cracker Crumbs [About 5 Crackers]
- 3 tbsp. Melted Unsalted Butter
- 1 tbsp. Sugar

Filling:

- 14-ounces can of Sweetened Condensed Milk
- ⅓ cup Sour Cream
- ½ cup Fresh Key Lime Juice
- 4 Large Egg Yolks
- 2 tbsp. Grated Key Lime Zest
- Whipped Cream [Optional]

Directions:

1. Prepare 7-inch springform pan by coating it with non-stick spray. In a small-sized bowl, combine graham cracker crumbs, butter and sugar. Press evenly into the bottom and up the side of pan. Place in the freezer for 10 minutes
2. In a large-sized mixing bowl, beat egg yolks until they are light yellow. Gradually beat in sweetened condensed milk until thickened. Gradually add lime juice and beat until smooth. Stir in sour cream and zest. Pour batter into the springform pan on top of crust. Cover top of springform pan with aluminum foil.
3. Pour 1 cup water into Instant Pot and place the trivet in the bottom. Carefully center the filled pan on a foil sling and lower it into Instant Pot. Fold the foil sling down so that it doesn't interfere with closing lid.
4. Lock lid in place. Select High pressure and set the timer for 15 minutes. When the beep sounds, turn off Instant Pot. Use a Natural pressure release for 10 minutes and then do a Quick pressure release to release any of the remaining pressure. When the valve drops carefully remove lid. Remove pie and check to see if the middle is set. If not, cook an additional 5 minutes
5. Remove the springform pan to a wire rack to cool. Remove the aluminum foil. When pie is cooled, refrigerate covered with plastic wrap for at least 4 hours. Top with whipped cream if so desired. Serve.

Chocolate Pots de Creme

[Servings: 6]

Ingredients:

- 8 ounces Melted Bittersweet Chocolate
- 5 Large Egg Yolks
- ¼ cup Sugar
- ½ cup Whole Milk
- 1 ½ cups of Water
- 1 ½ cups of Heavy Cream
- Pinch of Salt
- Whipped Cream [Optional]
- Grated Chocolate [Optional]

Directions:

1. In a small-sized saucepan, bring cream and milk to a simmer. In a large-sized mixing bowl, whisk together egg yolks, sugar and salt. Slowly whisk in hot cream and milk. Whisk in chocolate until blended. Pour into 6 custard cups.
2. Add 1 ½ cups of water to your Instant Pot and place trivet in the bottom. Place 3 cups on trivet and place second trivet on top of the cups. Stack the remaining 3 cups on top of the second trivet
3. Lock lid in place. Select High pressure and set the timer for 6 minutes. When the beep sounds, turn off your Instant Pot and use a Natural pressure release for 15 minutes and then do a Quick pressure release to release any of the remaining pressure. When the valve drops carefully remove lid. Carefully

remove the cups to a wire rack to cool uncovered. When cool, refrigerate covered with plastic wrap for at least 4 hours. Serve.

Dulce de Leche

[Servings: 4]

Ingredients:

- 14-ounce can of Sweetened Condensed Milk
- 16-ounce Canning Jar with Lid and Ring
- 8 cups of Water

Directions:

1. Pour sweetened condensed milk into a 16 ounce canning jar. Place the lid on jar and screw on the ring. Put a rack in your Instant Pot and place the jar filled on the rack. Add 8 cups of water. The water should reach half way up the jar
2. Lock the lid in place, select High pressure and 30 minutes cook time. When the timer beeps, turn off your Instant Pot and let the pressure release for 15 minutes. After 15 minutes, release any of the remaining pressure
3. Carefully remove the jar from Instant Pot. Allow the jar to cool for 10 minutes, then using a hot pad, open lid and whisk until smooth. Serve.

Fruit Yogurt

[Servings: 6]

Ingredients:

- 5 ⅔ cups of Organic Milk [Whole or Reduced-Fat]
- 2 cups of Fresh Fruit Chopped
- 4 Wide Mouth Pint Jars
- Plain Cultured Yogurt
- 4 tbsp. Non-Fat Dry Milk Powder
- 4 tbsp. All Natural Sugar
- 1 ½ cup Water

Directions:

1. Add 1 ½ cups of water to the bottom of your Instant Pot and add Grate. Put 1 ⅓ cup milk in each of jars. Place lids on loosely and place into Instant Pot
2. Pressure using the Pressure Cycle on your Instant Pot and reduce the time from 30 minutes to 2 minutes. This scalds the milk killing any pathogens that might be in the milk. Gives you a fresh clean slate to start with.
3. After cycle is done release steam from your Instant Pot and safely with a jar lifter remove the jars to cool. Remove lids carefully and place jars into cool water to speed up the cooling process
4. Once milk is below 100 degrees you can add yogurt culture safely to the milk. Add 1 tbsp. sugar to each jar.
5. Add 1 tbsp. non-fat dry milk to each jar. Add 1 tbsp. Yogurt Culture to each of jars and stir up the ingredients until mixed well
6. Add ½ cup fresh fruit to each jar. Be careful not to overfill jars. Leave at least 1/8-inch from the top of each jar. Replace lids and rings and place jars back into Instant Pot. Make sure it still has the 1 ½ cups of water in the bottom of Instant Pot.
7. Press the Yogurt cycle on your Instant Pot then increase the time from 8 hours to 12 hours. After the cycle is complete place them into refrigerator. Cooling it down will stop the cooking process by reducing the temperature. Serve.

Poached Pears with Chocolate Sauce

[**Servings:** 6]

Ingredients:

- 1 Lemon [Cut in Half]
- 6 Bartlett Pears [Ripe but Firm]
- 6 Cinnamon Sticks
- 3 cups of Water
- 2 cups of Organic Cane Sugar
- 2 cups of White Wine

Chocolate Sauce:

- 9 ounces of Bittersweet Chocolate [Cut in 1/2-Inch Pieces]
- ¼ cup Coconut Oil
- ½ cup Coconut Milk
- 2 tbsp. Maple Syrup or Honey

Directions:

1. Put water, sugar, wine and cinnamon sticks in Instant Pot. Select Sauté and bring to a simmer, stirring until sugar dissolves. Switch to the Keep Warm setting so the liquid stays hot until pears are peeled and ready.
2. Peel the pears, keeping them whole, with the stems intact. Rub them immediately with cut lemon to keep from turning brown. Squeeze the remaining lemon juice into wine/sugar syrup and drop juiced lemon into the syrup
3. Slip pears into the hot syrup, lock lid and bring to High pressure for 3 minutes. Quick release the pressure. Carefully remove pears with a slotted spoon and allow to cool. When syrup has cooled a bit, pour it over pears.
4. Place chocolate in a bowl. In a small-sized saucepan, over a medium flame, heat coconut milk, coconut oil and maple syrup to a boil. Pour it over chocolate and let it sit for a minute. Whisk until smooth. Keep warm until you serve pears
5. Slice a little piece off the bottom of each pear and so they will stand up. Place each pear on a plate and pour warm chocolate sauce over them. Serve.

Polenta

[**Servings:** 4]

Ingredients:

- 1 cup Polenta [Not Instant]
- 1 quart of Low Sodium Chicken Broth
- 2 tbsp. Butter or Olive Oil
- ½ tsp. Salt
- Olive Oil for Frying [Optional]

Directions:

1. Press the "Sauté" button on Instant Pot. Add chicken broth, butter and salt to pot. Bring it up to a simmer. When broth begins to simmer, pour polenta into the broth in a thin stream, whisking constantly to keep it from getting lumpy
2. Put the pressure cooker lid on Instant Pot and set the valve to "Sealing." Press the "Keep Warm/Cancel" button to reset Instant Pot. Then, press the "Porridge" button and adjust the time down to 8 minutes
3. When your Instant Pot beeps to signal the end of cooking, leave it on the "Keep Warm" setting for another 15 minutes.
4. After 15 minutes have passed, carefully turn the pressure valve to "Venting." When pressure has fully released, open your Instant Pot and remove the inner pot.
5. Stir with a wooden spoon to unstick any of the polenta that may be clinging to the bottom of pot. Taste for seasoning, adding more salt if necessary
6. You can either have the polenta as a porridge, or you can spread it out in a 1/2-inch layer on Silpat, allow it to cool to room temperature, then slice it into squares and fry in olive oil until golden brown. Should take about five minutes per side. Serve

Tapioca Pudding

[Servings: 4]

Ingredients:

- ⅓ cup Seed Tapioca Pearls
- ½ Lemon [Zested]
- ½ cup Sugar
- ½ cup Water
- 1 ¼ cups of Whole Milk

Directions:

1. Prepare your Instant Pot by adding 1 cup water and the steamer basket and set to the side. Rinse tapioca pearls in a fine-mesh strainer. To a 4-cup capacity heat-proof bowl, add tapioca pearls, milk, ½ cup water, lemon zest and sugar. Mix together well until sugar has dissolved and you no longer feel the grit of it at the base.
1. If container does not have handles to easily lower and lift it from Instant Pot, construct a foil sling. Lower heat-proof bowl into Instant Pot. Close and lock the lid. Cook for 8 minutes at High pressure.
2. When the time is up, open your Instant Pot with the Natural release method. Disengage the "keep warm" mode or unplug the cooker and open when the pressure indicator has gone down. Should take approximately 20 to 30 minutes
3. Once the pressure has released let mixture stand in the closed cooker for an additional 5 minutes before opening lid. The milk in container will boil over if you open the lid too quickly after the pressure is released.
4. Carefully lift out heat-proof bowl and vigorously stir with a fork before distributing into serving bowls, glasses, or forms. Cover tightly with cling wrap and allow it to cool before refrigerating for at least 3 hours, or overnight. Serve.

Cheese Flan

[Servings: 4]

Ingredients:

- 14-ounce can of Sweetened Condensed Milk
- 12-ounce of can of Evaporated Milk
- 5 Eggs
- 8-ounce of Cream Cheese Bar-Softened
- 6 tbsp. Sugar
- 1 tsp. Vanilla Extract
- Dash of Nutmeg
- Dash of Cinnamon

Directions:

1. Make caramel: Use flan pan to melt sugar. Stir until it is melted and a medium brown color. Don't allow it to burn. Remove from the heat and swirl the liquid sugar to coat the sides of pan. Make the custard while it cools
2. Put cream cheese in a medium-sized bowl. Add each egg one at a time until nicely blended. Add remaining ingredients and put in caramelized pan. Secure lid
3. Put a couple inches of water in your Instant Pot and place the flan on a trivet, cook it on manual for 15 minutes. Allow the pressure to drop naturally. Remove flan from your Instant Pot and let cool to room temperature. Refrigerate for 6 to 8 hours or longer if you want. Run knife around the edge of pan, flip onto a plate that has a rim to catch the caramel. Serve.

Robin Egg Mini Cheesecakes

[**Servings:** 6]

Ingredients:

Crust:

- 1 cup Graham Cracker Crumbs [8 Crackers]
- 1 tbsp. Sugar
- 3 tbsp. Melted Unsalted Butter

Filling:

- 12 ounces of Cream Cheese [Room Temperature]
- 1 Large Egg [Room Temperature]
- ¼ cup Granulated Sugar
- 2 tbsp. Sour Cream
- 1 cup Whoppers Robin Eggs Malted Milk Candies [Chopped]
- Pinch of Salt
- ½ tsp. Vanilla Extract
- Whipped Cream [Optional]
- Additional Robin Eggs for Decoration [Optional]

Directions:

1. Prepare six 6-ounce glass custard cups by spraying them with non-stick cooking spray. In a small-sized bowl, combine graham cracker crumbs, sugar and butter. Divide evenly between 6 custard cups. Press evenly into the bottom and up the side of pans about 1/2-inch. Place in freezer for 10 minutes.
2. In mixing bowl, mix cream cheese and sugar at a medium speed until smooth. Add vanilla, sour cream and salt and mix until blended. Add egg and mix until blended. Don't over mix. Gently fold in Robin Egg candies. Divide batter evenly between 6 cups
3. Pour 1 cup water into Instant Pot and place trivet in the bottom. Place 3 cups on the trivet. Place the second trivet on top of cups and place the remaining 3 cups on top.
4. Lock lid in place. Select High pressure and set timer for 5 minutes. When the beep sounds, turn off Instant Pot. Use a Natural pressure release for 10 minutes and then do a Quick pressure release to release any of the remaining pressure. When the valve drops carefully remove lid
5. Remove cups to a wire rack to cool. If necessary, remove any water drops from the top of cheesecake with a corner of paper towel. When cheesecake is cooled, refrigerate covered with plastic wrap for at least 4 hours. Add any additional Robin Egg candies for decoration or whipped cream. Serve

Heart Shaped Cheesecake

[**Servings:** 3]

Ingredients:

Crust:

- 1 cup Graham Cracker Crumbs [About 8 Crackers]
- 1 tbsp. Sugar
- 3 tbsp. Melted Unsalted Butter

Filling:

- 8-ounce package of Cream Cheese [Room Temperature]
- 1 Large Egg [Room Temperature]
- ¼ cup Granulated Sugar
- 2 tbsp. Sour Cream
- ½ tsp. Vanilla Extract
- Pinch of Salt

Triple Berry Sauce:

- 6 Large Fresh Strawberries [Diced]
- 1 cup Frozen Triple Berry Blend [Thawed]
- 2 tbsp. Sugar
- 3 tbsp. Water
- 1 tsp. Cornstarch

Directions:

1. Prepare three 4-inch heart-shaped springform pans by lining them with aluminum foil. In a small-sized bowl, combine graham cracker crumbs, butter and sugar. Divide evenly between the 3 pans. Press evenly into the bottom and up the side of the pans about 1/2-inch. Place in freezer for 10 minutes.
2. In a mixing bowl, mix cream cheese and sugar at a medium speed until smooth, blend in sour cream, vanilla and salt. Mix in egg until blended. Don't over mix. Divide batter evenly between the 3 springform pans on top of crust
3. Pour 1 cup water into Instant Pot and place the trivet in the bottom. Place 2 springform pans on the trivet. Place the second trivet on top of springform pans and place the third springform pan on top.
4. Lock lid in place. Select High pressure and set the timer for 6 minutes. When the beep sounds, turn off the Instant Pot. Use a Natural pressure release for 10 minutes and then do a Quick pressure release to release any of the remaining pressure. When the valve drops carefully remove lid
5. Remove springform pans to a wire rack to cool. If necessary, remove any water drops from the top of cheesecake with a corner of paper towel. When cheesecake is cooled, refrigerate covered with plastic wrap for at least 4 hours.
6. Add thawed berries and water to a small-sized saucepan. In a small-sized bowl, mix together sugar and cornstarch; add to saucepan and stir until dissolved. Bring to a boil over a medium-high heat, stirring constantly, until sauce thickens. Pour over diced strawberries in a mixing bowl and stir well to combine. Serve.

Berry Compote

[Servings: 2]

Ingredients:

- 2 cups of Sliced Fresh Strawberries
- 1 cup Blueberries
- ¾ cup Sugar
- 2 tbsp. Lemon Juice
- 1 tbsp. Water
- 1 tbsp. Cornstarch

Directions:

1. Add strawberries, ⅓ cup blueberries, sugar and lemon juice to Instant Pot. Stir well to combine. Lock lid in place and select High pressure and cook for 3 minutes. When the beep sounds turn off your Instant Pot and use a Natural pressure release for 10 minutes. After 10 minutes, release any of the remaining pressure with a Quick pressure release
2. In a small-sized bowl, whisk together cornstarch and water. Add to compote in Instant Pot. Bring to a boil using the Sauté function, stirring constantly. Stir in remaining blueberries. Put in a storage container and cool to room temperature. Refrigerate until ready to serve. Serve

Rice Pudding

[Servings: 8]

Ingredients:

- 1 ½ cups of Arborio Rice
- 1 cup Half and Half
- 1 cup Raisins
- 5 cups of 1% Milk
- ¾ cup Sugar
- 2 Eggs
- 1 ½ tsp. Vanilla Extract
- ½ tsp. Salt

Directions:

1. In Instant Pot, combine rice, milk, sugar and salt. Select Sauté and bring to a boil, stirring constantly to dissolve sugar. As soon as mixture comes to a boil, cover and lock the lid in place. Select Low pressure and set the timer for approximately 16 minutes
2. While rice is cooking, whisk eggs with half and half and vanilla. When the timer sounds, turn off Instant Pot, wait 10 minutes and then use a Quick pressure release. Carefully remove lid. Stir rice in the pot.
3. Stir egg mixture into the pot. Select Sauté and cook uncovered until mixture just starts to boil. Turn off Instant Pot. Stir in raisins
4. Pour into serving dishes. Cool then chill. Pudding will thicken as it cools, so you may want to add a little extra half and half if you're serving it cold. Serve.

Coconut Lemongrass Ginger Tapioca

[Servings: 8]

Ingredients:

- 1 cup Pearl Tapioca
- 1 cup Coconut Milk
- 4 cups of Coconut Milk Beverage
- 1 cup Sugar
- Smashed Lemongrass [6-Inch Piece]
- 2 tsp. Minced Fresh Ginger
- 4 Egg Yolks
- ½ tsp. Salt

Cashews:

- 2 tbsp. Sugar
- ½ tsp. Ground Cayenne Pepper
- ½ cup Cashews
- ½ tsp. Fine Sea Salt

To Finish:

- Crystallized or Sliced Candied Ginger
- Prepared Cashews
- Thai Basil Leaves

Directions:

1. Rinse pearl tapioca thoroughly. Add coconut milk beverage and pearl tapioca to Instant Pot. Use a mortar and pestle or meat tenderizer hammer to bruise lemongrass stalk. Add to your Instant Pot along with minced ginger
2. Lock lid in place. Bring to High pressure or select Rice setting. Cook for 6 minutes. Allow to depressurize for 10 minutes naturally. Release any of the remaining pressure.
3. Whisk sugar, egg yolks, salt, coconut milk and salt together. Whisk into tapioca. Return to a boil. Cool to room temperature. Once cooled, spoon into serving vessels and chill.
4. Prep the cashews. Add sugar to a small-sized saute pan over a medium-high heat. Cook until sugar melts. Add cashews. Using a wooden spoon, stir until coated. Add cayenne if using. Continue stirring until cashews begin to brown in spots
5. Scrape coated cashews onto a piece of foil or waxed paper. Sprinkle with sea salt. Garnish with thin slices of candied/crystallized ginger, cashews and chopped basil. Serve.

Steamed Bread Pudding

[Servings: 4]

Ingredients:

- 3 Eggs [Beaten]
- 1 cup Whole Milk
- 1 cup Goya Coconut Milk
- ½ cup Cranraisins
- 4 cups of Cubed Stale Bread
- 2 cups of Water
- 1 tsp. Cinnamon
- ½ tsp. Vanilla
- 1 tsp. Coconut Oil
- ¼ tsp. Salt

Directions:

1. Put 2 cups of water in your Instant Pot stainless steel inner pot. Add steam rack. Use a casserole dish small enough to fit into the Instant Pot, but large enough to hold bread and liquids. I use a casserole dish that is sloped up to 8-inches in diameter and 3-inches high
2. Cut bread in cubes. Mix the rest of ingredients in a bowl to combine. Put in cubed bread crumbs. Mix together well. Cover with wax paper and secure [I use silicone rubber bands that can withstand temperatures up to 600 degrees].
3. Set your Instant Pot to steam and adjust the time to 15 minutes. Allow the pressure to drop naturally. I usually wait an additional 15 minutes before removing the lid.
4. Remove casserole dish carefully. Remove wax paper and whatever secured it. Place it under a low broiler flame for about 5 to 8 minutes just to brown the top. Serve.

Raspberry Curd

[Servings: 2]

Ingredients:

- 12 ounces of Fresh Raspberries
- 1 cup Sugar
- 2 Egg Yolks
- 2 tbsp. Fresh Lemon Juice
- 2 tbsp. Butter

Directions:

1. Add raspberries, sugar and lemon juice to Instant Pot. Stir well to combine. Lock lid in place and select High pressure and 1 minute cook time
2. When the beep sounds turn off your Instant Pot and use a Natural pressure release for 5 minutes. After 5 minutes, release any of the remaining pressure with a Quick pressure release.
3. Use a food mill or fine mesh strainer to puree raspberries and remove seeds. In a small-sized bowl, whisk egg yolks. Gradually, whisk hot raspberry puree into the beaten egg yolks. Add mixture to the Instant Pot
4. Bring to a boil using the Sauté function, stirring constantly. Turn off Instant Pot. Stir in butter. Put in a storage container and cool to room temperature. Refrigerate until ready to serve. Serve.

Date Pumpkin Brown Rice Pudding

[Servings: 6]

Ingredients:

- 3 cups of Dairy-Free Milk
- ½ cup Water
- 1 cup Pumpkin Puree
- ½ cup Maple Syrup
- ½ cup Pitted Dates [Cut in Small Pieces]
- 1 cup Short Grain Brown Rice
- 1 stick of Cinnamon
- 1 tsp. Pumpkin Spice Mix
- 1 tsp. Vanilla Extract
- 1/8 tsp. Salt

Directions:

1. Cover rice with boiling water and allow it to sit for 10 minutes or up to an hour. Rinse. Bring milk and water to a boil in Instant Pot. Add soaked rice, dates, salt and cinnamon stick. Lock lid in place and bring to High pressure for 20 minutes. Use a Natural pressure release
2. When the pressure has released, stir in pumpkin puree, maple syrup and pumpkin spice mix. Cook, stirring constantly for 3 to 5 minutes, to thicken the pudding and cook out the raw pumpkin flavor. Remove from the heat and discard cinnamon stick. Stir in vanilla
3. Transfer to bowl and cover the surface with plastic wrap, so it touches the hot pudding, to prevent a skin from forming and so the steam from the hot pudding doesn't condense and create water on the surface. Allow it to cool for about 30 minutes. The pudding will thicken as it cools.
4. Spoon into serving cups. Top with maple-syrup sweetened coconut cashew whipped cream or fresh whipped cream. Sprinkle with pumpkin spice mix. Serve and enjoy!

Triple Chocolate Layered Cheesecake

[Servings: 16]

Ingredients:

Crust:

- 1 ½ cups of Chocolate Cookie Crumbs
- 4 tbsp. Melted Butter

Cheesecake Filling:

- 3 (8-ounce) packages of ⅓ Less-Fat Cream Cheese [Room Temperature]
- ½ cup Plain Greek Yogurt
- 4 ounces of Milk Chocolate
- 4 ounces of Bittersweet Chocolate
- 4 ounces of White Chocolate
- Sugared Cranberries [Optional]
- 3 Large Eggs [Room Temperature]
- 2 tbsp. Cornstarch
- 1 cup Sugar
- 1 tbsp. Vanilla Extract

Directions:

1. Spray deep dish 7-inch springform pan with nonstick cooking spray. Line the bottom of pan with parchment paper for easy removal of the cake once it's done. Stir cookie crumbs and melted butter together and press evenly across the bottom and halfway up the sides of pan. Place in freezer to set [this can be done 2 to 3 days in advance]
2. Cream cream cheese with a handheld mixer on low speed until very smooth. Scrape bowl and mix again. Add sugar and cornstarch; continue to scrape and mix the ingredients together on low speed until well combined and smooth. Add eggs, one at a time, continuing to mix and scrape bowl as needed. Finally, add yogurt and vanilla and mix just until blended. Scrape the bowl and continue to stir by hand until smooth, if needed.
3. Divide batter into 3 separate bowls [about 2 cups each]. Melt milk chocolate in the microwave for approximately 30 seconds, stir. Return chocolate to the microwave for another 15 to 30 seconds and stir until it is completely melted and smooth. Whisk into one of bowls of cheesecake batter. Repeat with

white and dark chocolate [each being stirred into a different bowl of batter]. Refrigerate the 3 bowls for 15 to 20 minutes so they will be more firm for layering.
4. Remove the bowls from fridge and take pan with the crust out of the freezer. Pour dark chocolate batter into the center of the crust and smooth to form an even layer. Very carefully spoon dollops of white chocolate batter on top of the dark chocolate, gently smooth over the top [gently so the layers don't mix together]. Repeat with milk chocolate batter
5. Add 1 cup water to your Instant Pot and place trivet inside. Carefully lower the prepared pan onto trivet. Secure the lid and turn pressure release knob to a sealed position. Cook at High pressure for 45 minutes.
6. When the pressure cooking is complete, use a 10-minute natural release and then release any of the remaining pressure.
7. Remove the pan from your Instant Pot and allow it to cool for 10 minutes. Slowly remove springform ring, being careful not to break the crust. Allow cake to cool completely and then cover and place in refrigerator for at least 4 hours.
8. Allow to stand at room temperature for approximately 30 to 60 minutes. Decorate with sugared cranberries, if so desired. Serve

Creme Brulee Cheesecake Bites

[Servings: 18]

Ingredients:

Cheesecake Crust:

- 8 Graham Crackers [Finely Ground]
- ¼ cup All-Purpose Flour [Optional]
- 4 tbsp. Melted Unsalted Butter
- 2 tsp. Brown Sugar
- Pinch of Sea Salt

Cheesecake Mixture:

- 16 ounces of Cream Cheese [Room Temperature]
- 2 Large Eggs [Room Temperature]
- ⅔ cup White Sugar
- 1/2 cup Sour Cream [Room Temperature]
- 2 tsp. Vanilla Extract
- 2 tbsp. Cornstarch
- Pinch of Sea Salt

Crackable Caramel:

- 2 tsp. White Sugar [Per Cheesecake Bite]

Directions:

1. Finely ground graham crackers in food processor or place graham crackers in a Ziploc bag, then roll them with rolling pin. In a small-sized mixing bowl, mix finely ground graham crackers, a pinch of sea salt and brown sugar together with fork. Mix in ¼ cup all-purpose flour if you are blind-baking the crust. Mix unsalted butter until the mixture sticks together
2. Place graham cracker crumbs into each silicone baking cups. Gently press down crumbs with a spoon to form a nice, even layer.
3. Place baking cups in the freezer while making the cheesecake mixture [Skip this step if you are baking the crust in the oven]
4. Optional - Blind-Bake the Cheesecake Crust: Place the baking cups in a 325°F oven for 12 to 15 minutes. Mix cornstarch, a pinch of sea salt and white sugar together.
5. In a medium-sized mixing bowl, beat cream cheese over a low speed with hand mixer until creamy. Add in half of sugar mixture and beat until incorporated using a low speed
6. Scrape down the sides and the hand mixer with a silicone spatula every time a new ingredient is added. Add remaining sugar mixture and beat until incorporated using a low speed.

7. Add sour cream and vanilla extract to the cream cheese mixture. Beat until incorporated using a low speed. Blend in eggs using a low speed, one at a time. Mix well after adding each egg. Try not to over mix on this step.
8. Scrape down the sides and the hand mixer with a silicone spatula and fold a few times to make sure everything is fully incorporated.
9. Fill baking cups to ⅔ full with cream cheese mixture. Tap the baking cups against the counter a few times to let the air bubbles rise to the surface. Burst air bubbles with a toothpick. Tap it a few more times until no air bubbles rise to the surface
10. Pour 1 cup cold running tap water into Instant Pot. Place the baking cups on top of trivet that doesn't touch the water. Close lid and pressure cook at High pressure for 7 minutes and full Natural release. The natural release will take roughly 7 minutes. Open lid carefully
11. Remove the baking cups from your Instant Pot and place them on a wire rack. After a few minutes, carefully run thumb against the rim of baking cups to avoid the cheesecake from sticking to the sides.
12. Once cheesecake baking cups have completely cooled, loosely cover them with aluminum foil. Then, place it in refrigerator for at least 4 to 6 hours
13. Carefully remove cheesecakes from the baking cups. Spread roughly 2 tsp. white sugar evenly on top of each cheesecake bite. Then, use a culinary torch to melt the sugar until it caramelizes evenly to form a hard crispy top. Serve.

Meyer Lemon Cheese cake

[Servings: 8]

Ingredients:

Crust:

- 8 ounces of Shortbread Cookies [About 10 Large Shortbread Cookies]
- 2 tbsp. Melted Butter

Filling:

- 2 (8-ounce) packages of Cream Cheese [Room Temperature]
- 2 Large Eggs
- ¼ cup Sour Cream
- ½ cup Granulated Sugar
- ½ tsp. Vanilla Extract
- 2 tsp. Grated Lemon Zest
- 1 tbsp. Meyer Lemon Juice

Directions:

1. Prepare a foil sling for lifting the pan out of your Instant Pot by taking an 18-inch strip of foil and folding it twice lengthwise. Set to the side
2. Crush cookies in a Ziploc bag into fine crumbs. Add butter and toss until well combined. Use fingers or the bottom of a drinking glass and press the crumbs evenly/firmly into the bottom and halfway up the sides of a 7-inch springform pan. Put pan in freezer until ready to use
3. In a large-sized mixing bowl, mix cream cheese and sugar until smooth. Add sour cream, Meyer lemon juice, vanilla, Meyer lemon zest and blend until well combined. Add in eggs one at a time and mix until combined. Do not over mix batter
4. Pour batter into springform pan on top of crumbs. Pour 1 cup water into your Instant Pot and place the trivet in the bottom. Carefully center the filled pan on foil strip and lower it into Instant Pot. Fold the foil strips down so that they do not interfere with closing lid.
5. Lock lid in place. Select High pressure and set the timer for 15 minutes for a soft creamy cheesecake or 25 minutes for a more firm, dense cheesecake. When the beep sounds, turn off your Instant Pot and use a Natural pressure release for 10 minutes and then do a Quick pressure release to release any of the remaining pressure. When the valve drops carefully remove lid
6. Remove pan to a wire rack to cool. If there is a little water on top blot with paper towel. When cheesecake is completely cooled, refrigerate covered with plastic wrap for at least 4 hours. Serve

Pumpkin Creme Brulee

[Servings: 6]

Ingredients:

- ⅓ cup Granulated Sugar
- ¼ cup Pumpkin Puree
- 6 Egg Yolks
- 2 cups of Heavy Cream
- 6 tbsp. Superfine Sugar
- 2 tbsp. Firmly Packed Light Brown Sugar
- 1 tsp. Vanilla Extract
- ¼ tsp. Pumpkin Pie Spice
- ½ tsp. Cinnamon
- Pinch of Salt

Directions:

1. Add 1 cup water to your Instant Pot and place trivet in the bottom.
2. In a large-sized mixing bowl with a pouring spout, whisk together egg yolks, granulated sugar, vanilla, brown sugar and pumpkin puree.
3. In a small-sized saucepan, whisk together heavy cream, cinnamon, salt and pumpkin pie spice. Heat over a medium heat until cream just begins to simmer
4. Whisking constantly, slowly pour warmed cream mixture into the egg mixture whisking until well blended. Pour mixture into 6 custard cups, cover with foil and place three on the trivet in Instant Pot. Add a second trivet and stack remaining 3 cups
5. Lock lid in place. Select High pressure and set the timer for approximately 6 minutes. When the beep sounds, turn off your Instant Pot and use a Natural pressure release for 15 minutes and then do a Quick pressure release to release any of the remaining pressure. When the valve drops carefully remove lid.
6. Carefully remove the cups to a wire rack to cool uncovered. When cool, refrigerate covered with plastic wrap for at least 2 hours or up to 2 days
7. Sprinkle a tbsp. sugar evenly over the top of each custard. Working with one at a time, move the flame of torch 2 inches above the surface of each custard in a circular motion to melt the sugar and form a crispy, caramelized topped. Serve.

Apple Sauce

[Servings: 4]

Ingredients:

- 10 Large Jonagold Apples [Peeled; Cored, and Quartered]
- ¼ cup Sugar
- ¼ cup Apple Juice
- 1 tsp. Ground Cinnamon

Directions:

1. Place apple pieces, apple juice, cinnamon and sugar in your Instant Pot and stir well to combine. Select High pressure and set cook time for 4 minutes
2. After the timer beeps, turn off Instant Pot. Wait 5 minutes and then use a Quick pressure release. Carefully remove lid. Use the Quick release method to release the pressure. Stir in apples, breaking up large chunks, until you've achieved desired consistency. Serve